CW01022763

The Girl from Tel Aviv

by Limi

The Girl from Tel Aviv

photography
MANOS CHATZIKONSTANTIS

food styling
LIMI ROBINSON

design
LESLEY GILMOUR

editor
JENNY LINFORD

SAVYONPRESS

To my dear sons
David, Yoeli and Srulik

המיצים של דוד
FRESH FRUIT JUICE
גזר תותים סלק תפוחים רימון
אשכולית אבטיח מלון תפוז
סלק גזר תפוח
רימון תפוז
גזר תפוח תפוז וג'ינגר
תפוח סלרי
מלבי נדיר
גזר תפוח
תפוז וג'ינג'ר
סלק גזר
תפוח וסלרי
יש ספירולינה
סלרי תפוח
עשב חיטה
אורגני
יש בקבוקים לקחת
לוינסקי 44
פרי הדר

CONTENTS

Introduction p.8

Taste of Tel Aviv p.12

Meal in a Bowl p.47

Delicious Dips & Rainbow Salads p.67

My Home by the Sea p.95

Quick & Easy p.119

My Kids Are Crazy For This p.151

Shabbat Shalom p.179

The Milky Way p.207

Balabuste in the Kitchen p.229

Tea-Time p.275

Delightful Desserts p.295

Drinks p.325

Sweet Memories p.339

Shalom Goodbye p.376

Notes & Tips p.392

Basics (Savoury & Sweet) p.383

Acknowledgements p.394

Index p.396

INTRODUCTION

WHY I WROTE THIS BOOK

When I think back to my childhood, I bask in precious memories of Tel Aviv, the city where I was born. I recall the bright, warm sunlight, the distinctive Bauhaus buildings, the white shutters on the windows, the rich variety of food and cultures, the shouts of market vendors and the smells. In almost every backyard grew bright yellow groundsel flowers. I still miss Old Jaffa with its ancient port, the beach with its soft, white sand and the infinite blue sea.

Food fills my memories of that time. As a child everything was new to my palate and seemed to taste better than food does today. When I married and moved to London, I was happy to finally cook on my own, with my mother instructing me on every step over the phone! I started cooking the dishes I remembered from Tel Aviv. My husband and my sons have always enjoyed and appreciated my cooking. When my son was six, he asked me anxiously: 'Mummy, what happens if when I marry, my wife doesn't know how to cook the same food you do?' I replied with a smile, 'Don't worry, I'll write my recipes down for you in a book.' It was the kernel of an idea and with my husband's encouragement I started to think seriously about it.

Once I had decided to write a cookbook, I did a lot of research. I got recipes from my mother, aunts, friends in Israel and neighbours in Stamford Hill, tracking down original methods and working away on dishes until I was satisfied. I spent hours talking to my mother to learn how to re-create the dishes I loved most. It took a lot of work but I am a persistent person. I always knew, too, that this wouldn't be just a cookbook — a simple collection of recipes — because I have a story to tell. The story of my beloved Tel Aviv and my vibrant childhood back then in the '70s.

I never thought that it would take four years! There's so much work involved, from testing the recipes repeatedly, finding the best ingredients, buying props and cooking each recipe myself for the photoshoot (often more than once!). It was exhausting but rewarding. I couldn't have made it without the constant encouragement of my husband, children and professional team.

THE POWER OF FOOD

We often think of food as an energy source, a way to satisfy physical hunger but its role is far larger than that. Food is a person's biography — signifying your roots, background and culture. It fills the soul, calms and comforts us. It is a magnet which draws people together. Home cooking is central to family life. To cook food for your children nourishes both body and soul.

In Hebrew the word 'lisod' means to feed, help and support. In Jewish communities, whenever a neighbour or a friend comes back from abroad, they are greeted with

fresh bread, milk and pastries. New mothers receive a cheesecake as well as meals for the first week after a child is born. New neighbours too are presented with the gift of freshly baked cakes. When I first arrived at Stamford Hill in London, it warmed my heart to receive such a welcome.

Food is our comfort in times of sorrow or loss. Whenever somebody in our community is ill, neighbours will bring them freshly cooked meals. When a family has been bereaved, friends and neighbours bring food with them whenever they visit. This powerful association begins in childhood, from the first moment a child is cheered up with a sweet treat or biscuit.

As a child I was absolutely petrified of needles (I still am!). I used to shake with fear whenever I went for a blood test. The nurses would say: 'Don't worry: just think, in the Holocaust they suffered more.' That's how they calmed children in those days. After the ordeal, my mother consoled me with a 'baygele' (pretzel) and a chocolate drink from a small stall outside the surgery. To this day, I feel comforted whenever I eat a pretzel.

THE KOSHER COOK: A MAGICIAN IN THE KITCHEN

You need to be a magician to cook tasty Kosher food because there are so many restrictions. Judaism prohibits eating pork or shellfish and permits only fish that have scales. Furthermore, Sephardi and the Ashkenazi communities have different customs when it comes to cuisine and both can use only Kosher ingredients. The various Jewish festivals involve cooking specific dishes, with Passover particularly challenging from a cook's perspective, with strict rules covering flour, pasta and bread (even extended to the use of certain oils, pulses, rice and corn).

We can't use dairy and meat products in the same dish, so no frying steaks in butter for me! After eating meat, we can't eat dairy for six hours. So, if I'm planning a dinner party, I have to bear this in mind when it comes to desserts. We can't eat dishes that contain both meat and fish so if I make paella, it's with either fish or chicken. Another important thing is not to eat any insects. This is considered even worse than eating pork! Before cooking we have to wash and check all our fresh produce very carefully indeed to make sure that it doesn't contain any little bugs. Certain vegetables like broccoli or cauliflower are particularly hard to check so we often buy them frozen, having been cleaned and inspected.

Perhaps these limitations help us to be more creative in the kitchen. For example, instead of frying a steak in butter, I melt lamb fat instead (a great trick that my mum showed me). For dessert after a meat course I make ice cream using coconut milk instead of cream.

When I came to London, it was torture to walk through the streets of the West End. I was surrounded by an abundance of restaurants, coffee shops and bakeries, the tantalising aroma of food all around me which I wasn't allowed to eat. I looked enviously at the happy customers enjoying moist carrot cake, golden fried fish and crispy chips with tartare sauce and succulent aromatic chicken curry. It was so frustrating. One day I resolved to cook those enticing dishes that were so new to me for us to enjoy at home. Now, the happy customers are sitting at my kitchen table!

The restrictions and frustrations that I have endured have resulted in the recipes in this book, the product of cooking countless meals, of considerable time and experimentation. So, after all, it is possible to cook Kosher food without compromising on quality and flavour. With this book, I hope to share the magic of my memories, stories and kitchen with you.

THE FIRST TIME I EVER COOKED

I was nine years old, staying with my friend Orit in Tel Aviv. She lived in a big, posh flat which had a modern kitchen — the first time I had ever seen such a large kitchen — and her family had a colour TV! I always wanted to visit her home.

One evening, while her parents were away, she and her brothers wanted to make supper. They asked me if I knew how to cook. As I wanted to impress them, I said 'oh yes', at once, even though all I had ever done was watch my mother cook. I made them omelettes and — inspired by the blintzes my mum made — I put soft white cheese and green olives in the middle of each omelette and folded it over like a blintz. My other culinary creation which they loved was my inspired suggestion of the Ketchup Toast sandwich (as I'd just discovered tomato ketchup). As a result, I was often invited over, especially at suppertime.

THE SPECIAL 'INGREDIENT'

My most vivid childhood memories are of food. All five senses are involved when you eat which triggers powerful memories and emotions. One bite into a pastry or a spoonful of a soup can awaken distant recollections and feelings.

I remember walking home from primary school for lunch, the main meal of the day in Israel. I would think about my mum's food on my way, wondering happily about the menu. Was it going to be stuffed peppers or juicy steak and her amazing chips (fries)? Would it be crispy schnitzel with soft mashed potato or a yummy kebab? Or maybe her amazing grilled chicken with its perfect crispy skin?

Supper was a lighter meal. Mum would serve us food in special trays with compartments: avocado, boiled eggs or omelette, salad, and, most importantly, a toasted cheese sandwich spread with a generous amount of butter, the proper way! How tasty those times were without health awareness!

Love is the special 'ingredient' that parents add when they cook for their children. The connective power of the food a parent makes for their family is immeasurably important, forming unforgettable childhood memories. Were somebody else to cook the same dishes and follow the same recipes, it wouldn't taste the same as your parent's cooking because it lacks that special ingredient.

my dad,
outside the townhall

Dad in Allenby St

My kindergarten New Year greetings card

Taste of Tel Aviv

GROWING UP IN TEL AVIV IN THE 1970S

My family and I lived in Tel Aviv, in Ezrah-Hasofer Street, until I was eleven and a half. We were close to Jaffa and just a minute from the sea. The majority of Israel's urban population lived in flats in those days. The wealthy lived in houses but the fun of living in a block was that there were so many other children to play with.

I have a deep affection for our childhood home. It was a three-story building with white shutters. We lived on the first floor in a flat which was spacious and airy. I remember walking along the long corridor with its geometric patterned tiles on the floor. The kitchen had red and yellow cupboards and the dining room a yellow-checked Formica table and chairs. The bedroom which I shared with my brothers and sisters had pink and red curtains and a bunkbed. As the oldest, I had the top bunk. So cool. I used to lie on my bunk and stare at the curtains which had a graphic pattern that made me think of eyes. In the summer we slept under light, textured, cotton piqué blankets. Whenever we woke up in the morning, we had the waffle pattern of the blankets imprinted on our cheeks! I loved our living room with its wood panelled wall, the bamboo sofa with floral patterned cushions, our gramophone, a big, dark red Persian rug and a balcony which looked out over the sea. It was a peaceful, inviting space. On a winter's day the orange curtains at the large windows spread warm light across the room.

An image that stays with me is of the washing lines hung with towels outside the flats all around us. On these towels you could read the names of the best hotels in Israel: Hilton, Sheraton, Plaza.... Whenever anyone stayed at a hotel, it was the practice to take a towel home as a 'souvenir'. Hanging them out on your washing line was the perfect way to show the world how many hotel towels you had.

NOTHING BAD CAN HAPPEN!

I guess we felt immortal in 1970s Israel. It was as though 'nothing bad can happen'. We didn't worry about smoking. We used margarine and MSG, enjoyed lots of sweets, red meat and fizzy drinks. We didn't use sun cream or wear seat belts. Children as young as six were allowed to go to school on their own. They pedalled their bikes all around town — without helmets.

Life had a slower pace, full of content and meaning. We weren't glued to screens. After school we played outdoors in the streets of the neighbourhood — games like: skipping, hopscotch, ball games and a jumping game using a long rubber band.

My mum didn't have an electric stand mixer or a food processor yet there were always delicious cakes in the fridge. We lived without a tumble dryer, vacuum cleaner or colour TV. We only got a phone line when I was nine. We didn't have hundreds of ice cream flavours, countless toys or computer games (in fact, we didn't have computers). It feels as if parents were calmer and children were happier. Life was blissful back then!

I was the oldest of five children with two sisters and two brothers. Us kids shared one big bedroom. We had only a few toys so we appreciated what we had. I remember my doll had a pimple on its face. My favourite toy was a soft stuffed black chimpanzee. I used to dress it up in baby clothes and pretend it was a baby. We built Lego houses, played snakes and ladders and when we were given colouring pens — which were expensive — we would draw for hours. It was fashionable to collect things: stamps, pretty stationery sets, even napkins.

I spent my first and second grade at The Balfour School. It was a wonderful place. I had many friends and a great teacher named Mrs Tova. She loved me because I was such a bookworm. I already knew how to read when I arrived and Mrs Tova used to call me to the blackboard from time to time to teach the class!

The Balfour School encouraged students to be creative. The corridor walls were covered with colourful works of art made by the students. There was a school newspaper that each of us could write in, a few lines every week.

My favourite pastime was to read. I was fast, devouring a book a day if I got the chance. I was the only student to whom the school librarian lent two books at a time. My favourite tales were by Hans Christian Andersen, especially *The Little Match Girl*. It was so sad and moving that I cried every time I read it.

I was curious to learn about the world. In those days, vendors went door to door to sell huge sets of encyclopaedias for both children and adults. I persuaded my parents to buy books from them which I would read over and over, fascinated by the world of knowledge. I still prefer books to jewellery: for me, books are more precious than gems.

One stop shop
03-5238740
PetBuy לחיות מחמד
אליה אורטופדיק
קסם בעיר
110
מוניסור מחשבים
03-5-299-299
מוניטור

TUNA FOCACCIA

MAKES 6 PORTIONS

- 1 focaccia loaf, home-made (see p.386) or shop-bought
- 3 small (160g/5oz) cans of tuna in oil, drained
- 4–5 large romaine lettuce leaves, central stalk removed, halved lengthways and cut into thin shreds
- 1 tbsp mayonnaise
- 1 tbsp ketchup
- Salt and pepper
- 1 onion, halved lengthways, then sliced finely
- Olive oil, for drizzling

PINK SAUCE

- 2 tbsp mayonnaise
- 5 tbsp ketchup

TOPPING (OPTIONAL)

- 6 tomato slices
- 3 gherkins, finely sliced

Pizza Pacha

Preheat oven to 190°C/375°F.

Trim the crusts off the focaccia to turn the oval loaf into a rectangular shape without any hard crust edges. Cut the trimmed loaf into six even-sized pieces. Slice each piece across as you would for a sandwich, and set the upper (crusty) pieces aside.

In bowl, thoroughly mix together the tuna, lettuce, mayonnaise and ketchup, seasoning with salt and pepper. Spread the tuna mixture over the six remaining focaccia pieces.

Place the tuna-topped slices on a baking paper-lined oven tray. Top the tuna with onion slices. Place the remaining slices crust-side down alongside.

Drizzle olive oil over both the topped and untopped bread pieces. Bake for 15–20 minutes (until the onion has slightly charred).

In the meantime, make the pink sauce by mixing together the mayonnaise and ketchup, thinning with 1–2 tbsp water if desired.

Remove the baked focaccia from the oven. Top each tuna-topped slice with a piece of tomato, sliced gherkin and pink sauce, and cover with a crusty slice. Place each tuna sandwich in a foil bag or wrap tightly in foil so that the flavours can blend. Set aside to cool slightly, then serve warm.

During the 1990s, when I was working in Tel Aviv, a new little Italian pizzeria called Pizza Pacha opened up nearby. I was their first customer! This is where I tried proper calzone and pizza for the first time. One of my favourites was their amazing Tuna Focaccia sandwich, which they slightly charred in a tabun (a wood-burning oven) to give it a smoky flavour. When I left Israel, I missed this sandwich so much that I worked out the recipe so that I could enjoy a taste of Tel Aviv in London!

SHAWARMA

SERVES 8

750g (1lb 10oz) boneless, skinless chicken thighs, finely sliced into strips
750g (1lb 10oz) boneless lamb cutlets or chops, finely sliced into strips
Coarsely ground black pepper
50g (2oz) lamb fat
2 onions, halved and sliced

MARINADE
Generous 5 tbsp olive oil
Generous 5 tbsp sunflower oil
1 tsp garam masala
1 tbsp mild curry powder
½ tsp ground baharat
¼ tsp ground cardamom
1 tbsp honey
1 tbsp chicken stock powder
¼ tsp garlic powder (optional)

FOR SERVING
Pitta
Perfect Chips (see p.388)
Israeli Salad (see p.82)
Runny Tahini Dip (see p.190)
Shifka (pickled hot peppers)

TIP: I like to use a mixture of chicken and lamb, but you can use just one of those meats if you prefer. To make the raw chicken and lamb easier to slice, I like to firm it up by half-freezing it.

Mix all the marinade ingredients in a large bowl. Add chicken and lamb and season with coarsely ground black pepper. Using your hands, mix the ingredients firmly together. Cover and marinate in the fridge for at least 2 hours or overnight.

Heat a wide, heavy sauté pan over a low heat. Add the lamb fat and fry it in the pan until browned and melted. Increase the heat to medium high. Add half the marinated meat mixture and half of the sliced onion. Fry, stirring with a wooden spoon, until just cooked and lightly singed. Remove from the pan and set aside. Spoon off the excess fat. Fry the remaining meat and onion in same way. Add the first batch to the pan, mix the two batches together and warm through briefly.

Serve the Shawarma in pitta with Perfect Chips (fries) (see p.388), Israeli Salad (see p.82) and runny Tahini Dip (see p.190) or with white rice instead of pitta and chips (fries). Serve pickled hot peppers (Shifka) on the side.

Everywhere you go in Israel you find Shawarma. It's street food at its best. Who wouldn't prefer a mouth-watering, tasty Shawarma to a Michelin-starred meal? A good Shawarma should be juicy, thanks to the lamb fat. The spicing should be aromatic but well-balanced. This recipe is for my home-made version, the closest I could get to an authentic Shawarma. It's a trusty formula to make my husband happy!

love life. love...
Jaffa
love life. love...
Jaffa

SABICH

SERVES 6

CRISPY FRIED AUBERGINE (EGGPLANT)

3 large aubergines (eggplant), sliced lengthways 1.5cm (around ½ in) thick
Salt and pepper
Flour for coating
Cornflour (corn starch) for coating
Oil for frying

TO SERVE

6 laffa bread (see p.387) or large pitta
Runny Tahini Dip (see p.190)
Hummus (see p.68)
6 hard-boiled eggs or Huevos Haminados (see p.385), shelled and sliced
4 boiled potatoes, peeled, cut into 1cm slices, and seasoned with salt and pepper while still warm
A large handful of parsley leaves
1 bunch of spring onions (scallions), finely sliced, or 1 red onion, sliced
Gherkins, sliced
Preserved lemons, sliced (see p.389)
2 tomatoes, sliced
Zhoug (see p.70)
Amba (pickled mango condiment)
Sumac or ground cumin

Prepare and cook the aubergine (eggplant): Sprinkle the slices with salt on both sides. Place in a colander over a bowl and set aside for at least 2 hours to draw out excess moisture and bitterness. Lightly pat the slices dry with kitchen paper.

Mix even quantities of flour and cornflour (corn starch) together. Dip the aubergine slices in the flour mixture, coating both sides, and lightly shake off the excess.

Heat oil in deep frying pan to a depth of 2cm (¾in) over medium-high heat. Fry the aubergine (eggplant) in batches until golden on both sides. Drain on kitchen paper.

Assemble the Sabich: Spread each laffa with tahini and hummus (using either or both as you want), top with freshly cooked, crispy fried aubergine (eggplant), then hard-boiled egg and potato slices. Season with salt and pepper and add other toppings as you want.

Fold up the lower quarter of the laffa over the filling, then roll over from the side to form a filled pocket. Serve at once.

TIP: The fried aubergine (eggplant) must be warm. If it's not warm and crisp, it's not proper Sabich.

"When my sons eat Sabich, it satisfies all their gastronomic desires in one bite."

THE STORY OF ISRAELI FALAFEL

The falafel comes originally from Egypt, where it is made from peeled broad beans (called *foul*). When the Egyptian Jews arrived in Israel they couldn't find peeled broad beans, so instead they used peeled chickpeas, which were widely available. To this day, Israeli falafel are made from chickpeas. Even though broad beans are now widely available, there is only one place in Tel Aviv where one can find Egyptian-style falafel made from broad beans — a tiny, tiny shop called Rahmo Hagadol (big Rahmo) which sells amazing falafel.

Today falafel has travelled around the world and is regarded as Israel's national dish. It was an Israeli inspiration to put falafel in pitta bread, which for me is the best way to eat them. In other parts of the Middle East, falafel are traditionally served on a plate or in wraps.

Another classic Israeli touch is to combine falafel with sauerkraut. Historically, in Israel next to the Egyptian Jewish stalls selling falafel were Ashkenazi stalls selling hotdogs with sauerkraut. With classic Israeli culinary creativity, the two traditions met and combined. Nowadays, falafel in Israel is served in a pitta filled with sauerkraut, Israeli salad and tahini dip — a wonderful combination of flavours and textures.

GREEN FALAFEL

MAKES AROUND 40

FALAFEL

500g (1lb 2oz) dried chickpeas
1 tsp bicarbonate of soda
1 onion, peeled and quartered
3 spring onions (scallions), roughly chopped
10–11 garlic cloves, peeled
1 hot green chilli, deseeded and scraped
30g (1oz) fresh parsley leaves, chopped
100g (3½ oz) fresh coriander leaves, chopped

SEASONING

1½ tbsp ground cumin
2 tbsp sesame seeds
1 tbsp ground coriander
1¼ tbsp salt
1 tsp bicarbonate of soda
2 tsp chickpea (gram) flour

6 tbsp water

Oil, for deep frying

FOR SERVING

Pitta
Puffy Falafel Chips (see p.388)
Runny Tahini Dip (see p.190)
Sauerkraut
A mixture of tomato and cucumber, finely chopped
Shifka (pickled hot peppers)

Soak the chickpeas: Rinse the chickpeas and place in a large bowl. Cover well with water, to a height of around 10cm (4in) above the chickpeas, and add the bicarbonate. Cover and set aside to soak for 20 hours, then drain and rinse well.

Make the falafel: Place half of the falafel ingredients in a food processor. Process in short bursts, scraping down the sides often, until finely chopped, then transfer to a large bowl. Repeat with the remaining ingredients.

Add the seasoning ingredients and water and mix thoroughly with your hands. Taste to check the seasoning and adjust as required. Cover and chill in the fridge for 1–2 hours.

Heat the oil in a deep saucepan over medium heat.

Meanwhile, with oiled hands shape the falafel mixture into ping pong-sized balls. I like to flatten the balls slightly on two sides. as this shape cooks better inside and becomes very crispy.

Cook the falafel: Test that the oil is hot enough by placing a wooden spoon handle-side down in the oil. If small bubbles form around the handle, the oil is ready. I like to first add just one falafel and fry it until browned on all sides, then remove it.

Fry the remaining falafel in batches, turning as required with a slotted spoon. Once they are browned on all sides, remove with a slotted spoon and drain in a colander. Bear in mind that these falafel will be darker because of the herbs.

Serve the falafel in pitta with Puffy Falafel Chips (see p.388), runny Tahini Dip (see p.190), sauerkraut, salad and pickled hot peppers (Shifka) on the side.

For years I wondered why I couldn't make falafels that tasted as good as the ones I bought in falafel bars. I tried numerous recipes, which all required using a mincer for the chickpea mixture. Then one day, by accident, I cracked it. My mincer was broken, so I used my food processor instead. I was thrilled with the results! My falafel were crisp on the outside, soft and moist inside and flavoured with herbs.

SHAKSHUKA

SERVES 6

2 tbsp olive oil
40g (4 tbsp) butter
1 onion, chopped (optional)
1 hot green or red chilli, sliced
7 garlic cloves, sliced or chopped
500g (1lb 2oz) cherry tomatoes, quartered
Salt and pepper
6 eggs
2 tbsp chopped parsley or coriander
50g (2oz) feta cheese, crumbled (optional)
Bread or pitta, to serve

TIP: For a quick version, use a few tbsp of Matbukha (see p.73) as the base and simply add eggs to it.

Heat the oil and butter together in a large lidded frying pan over medium heat. Add onion (if using) and fry until lightly golden.

Add the chilli and fry, stirring often, for 1 minute. Add the garlic, mixing in, and fry for 30 seconds. Add the cherry tomatoes. Season with salt and pepper. Taste and adjust as required.

Reduce the heat to low, cover and cook for 5 minutes until the tomatoes have softened.

Break one of the eggs into a small bowl. Use a spoon to make a hollow in the tomato mixture and pour in the egg. Repeat the process until all the eggs are nestled in the pan. Sprinkle with the parsley. If using feta, dot the cheese between the eggs.

Cover and cook over a low heat for 10–15 minutes, until the eggs feel firm and have a white film on top.
Serve with bread or pitta.

> "For me this is the 'omelette' of the Middle East — originally from North Africa, but now part of Israeli food culture."

Dr Shakshuka Restaurant, Jaffa

GREEN SHAKSHUKA

SERVE 4

325g (around 11oz) spinach leaves
40g (4 tbsp) butter
Salt and pepper
4 eggs
90g (3oz) feta cheese
Olive oil, to serve

Put the spinach in a bowl and cover with boiling water. Leave for 5 minutes, drain, squeeze dry and coarsely chop.

Melt the butter over a medium heat in a medium lidded frying pan. Add the spinach, season with salt and pepper, mixing in.

Break each egg into a small bowl. Use a spoon to make a hollow in the spinach. Pour an egg into the hollow. Repeat the process, until all the eggs are nestled in the pan.

Dot chunks of feta onto the spinach around the eggs. Season with black pepper. Reduce the heat to very low, cover the pan and cook for 10 minutes, until the eggs feel firm and have a white film on top.

Drizzle the shakshuka with a little olive oil and serve with bread.

"This spinach shakshuka is so quick and easy, perfect for a tasty breakfast. I love it!"

BBQ TIPS

In Israel, we take barbecuing very seriously, so let me share a few useful tips:

- Always use flat metal skewers for shishlik or kebab. The metal heats up and helps cook the inside of the meat.
- When you want to take the shishlik meat off the skewer, use a piece of pitta to push it off — easy!
- There is no better match for chicken shishlik than Toum (see p.79) or Tahini Dip (see p.190).
- Use half an onion to wipe your barbecue grill just before cooking on it— this gives a great flavour to the food.

CHICKEN SHISHLIK

SERVES 6

12 boneless, skinless chicken thighs, cut into 5 x 7.5cm (2 x 3in) pieces
300g (10oz) lamb fat, cut into 3 x 1cm (around 1 x ⅓in) squares
2 onions, sliced into square-ish pieces (optional)

MARINADE
5 tbsp olive oil
Juice of 1 lemon
2 garlic clove, crushed (optional)
1 tsp sugar
1 tsp baharat
1 tsp paprika
1 tsp curry powder
Pinch of turmeric
1 tsp garam masala
Salt and pepper

TO SEASON THE BARBECUE
Half an onion
Oil, for brushing

TO SERVE
Pitta or Laffa (see p.387)
Toum (see p.79) or Tahini Dip (see p.190)
Grated tomato with Zhoug (see p.70)

Mix the marinade ingredients in a large bowl. Add the chicken and mix thoroughly with your hands. Cover and marinate in the fridge for 2 hours.

Prepare the barbecue. Heat the coals until they are white-hot and glow red when fanned.

On flat, wide metal skewers, thread alternate pieces of chicken, lamb fat and onion, if using.

Pierce half an onion firmly on a fork, flat-side down, brush it lightly with oil and use the onion to oil the barbecue rack just before you place the chicken on the rack. This gives the barbecued food a delicious onion flavour.

Cook the chicken skewers on the barbecue, turning them to ensure they cook evenly. Once cooked through, serve immediately with pitta, grated tomato with zhoug, and toum or tahini dip.

In Israel, the term 'shishlik' is used to describe pieces of meat cooked on a skewer, while 'kebab' is for minced meat on a skewer. In Britain, I discovered, the terms are the other way around. I don't know when the custom of eating food cooked on a mangal (barbecue grill) to celebrate Israeli Independence Day began. What I do know, though, is that if you're in Israel on that day, all the parks are filled with people busy fanning the coals on their barbecues while the air smells temptingly of grilling meat. It's the most amazing, surreal sight. I don't know where in the world you could find so many people barbecuing at once — we could set a Guinness World Record.

Calf foot soup 35
תבשיל בשר, תפוח
אורז ושעועית
35

Albert S. Ruddy
The Godfather
Marlon Brando
Al Pacino
James Caan Richard Castellano Robert Duvall
Sterling Hayden John Marley Richard Conte Diane Keaton
שמן זית

RAINBOW SWEETS & PITTA

I was a curious girl who liked to explore everything, so I loved my walk to school and would always dawdle on my way. I would pause in the doorway of the huge pitta bread bakery, drawn by the smell of baking, to watch the circular conveyor belt carrying hundreds of packets of freshly baked pitta breads. One day the bakery owner noticed me and asked 'Would you like a pitta?' He probably assumed that I was poor and hungry, because I was so skinny. I nodded. From then on, he gave me a warm pitta every morning.

Next, I strolled through Carmel Market just as dozens of vendors were opening their stalls, busily setting up displays of fresh fruit, herbs, cold lemonade, toys and clothing. My favourite stall was the one selling rainbow-coloured blocks of stripy jelly sweets — a sight which still excites me to this day!

OUR HAMBURGER

SERVES 8

I use a mixture of beef and lamb for flavour, but you can use only beef if you wish.

500g (1lb 2oz) minced (chopped) beefsteak
500g (1lb 2oz) minced lamb chops
1 red onion finely chopped
1–2 tbsp soy sauce
Salt and pepper
Oil for coating and frying

THE TOPPINGS
Mayonnaise
Iceberg or Romaine lettuce, shredded
Barbecue sauce
Ketchup
American mustard
Crispy fried onion (see p388)
Tomato slices
Gherkin slices

TO SERVE
8 burger buns
Coleslaw salad (see p.87)
Chips (fries) (see p.388)

Make the burgers: In a bowl, mix together well the minced beef, lamb, red onion, and soy sauce. Season with salt and pepper. Divide into 8 equal portions and with oiled hands shape each portion into 1cm (around ⅓ in thick) patties, roughly the size of your hamburger buns.

Add 1 tbsp oil to the frying pan, spreading it evenly, and heat over medium heat. Fry the patties in batches. Space each batch of patties well apart and fry for 2 minutes, turn, and fry for a further 2 minutes. Set aside the fried patties and repeat the process until they have all been fried. You may need to add more oil if the pan is getting dry.

Spoon off the excess oil and reheat the pan over medium heat. Halve the burger buns. Briefly char the halves, white side down, pressing them down onto the pan. If the pan becomes too dry, add a little more oil.

To assemble each burger, take the bottom half of a freshly charred bun, spread a little mayonnaise in the middle, and top with shredded lettuce. Add the burger, then top with barbecue sauce, ketchup or mustard to your taste. Layer with crispy fried onion, tomato and gherkin slices, then top with the top half of the burger bun. I like to use a short bamboo skewer to hold the burger together. Repeat the process and serve the burgers at once with coleslaw and chips (fries).

MacDavid was one of the first burger bars in Israel, opened in Tel Aviv in 1978. Some of the burgers on the menu were named in tribute to Abie Nathan and his Peace Ship. The MacDavid Abie burger with fried onions was the best. I was so sad when the original McDavid closed — I miss those burgers to this day! I haven't been able to recreate the Abie burger exactly — as no one can make them the same way — but these come close.

SAMIS' BOUREKAS

MAKES 10 BOUREKAS

1kg (2lb 4oz) good-quality puff pastry sheets, preferably butter puff pastry*

FILLING

300g (10½ oz) good quality Bulgarian or feta cheese, crumbled

100g (3½ oz) Emmenthal cheese, finely grated

2 tbsp soft white cheese, such as Quark

1 small potato, peeled, boiled, and mashed while warm

1 egg

Salt and pepper

GLAZE

1 egg, beaten

2–3 tsp sesame seeds

*If you can't find butter puff pastry, before filling, brush each pastry square in the middle lightly with melted butter, to give a richer flavour.

Preheat the oven to 180°C/350°F. Line two baking trays with baking parchment. Cut the puff pastry sheets into 10 squares, approximately 13cm (5in) square. Mix together the three cheeses, cooled mashed potato and egg. Season with salt and pepper, mixing well.

Place 1 heaped tbsp of the cheese filling in the centre of each pastry square. Fold the pastry over the filling to form triangular parcels, pressing the edges down to seal well.

Place the parcels on the baking trays with plenty of space between them. Brush with the beaten egg, being careful not to brush right to the edge of the bourekas. Sprinkle with sesame seeds.

Bake in the oven for 20–25 minutes until golden. Serve warm from the oven.

The sight of bourekas always makes me think of Sami's. When I was a little girl growing up in Tel Aviv, my father would often take us at weekends to Jaffa to have breakfast at Sami Bourekas. This was a small, bustling place filled with checked Formica tables. There we would eat the most wonderful, crisp, cheese-filled bourekas, served freshly baked from the oven on a tray with hard-boiled eggs, Israeli salad and a tall glass of delicious hot chocolate. The smell when we entered was so inviting and the bourekas we ate there were one of my favourite childhood treats. After eating them, we'd be covered in crumbs and very happy.

לחמנייה עגולה חומה
1 – 2 שח
10 – 10 שח
לחמניות קמח מלא
1 יח – 3 שח
6 יח – 10 שח
חדש לחם אישי לבן
1 – 5 שח
3 – 12 שח
חלבי

אטליז
שערי הלכה
054-8400-406

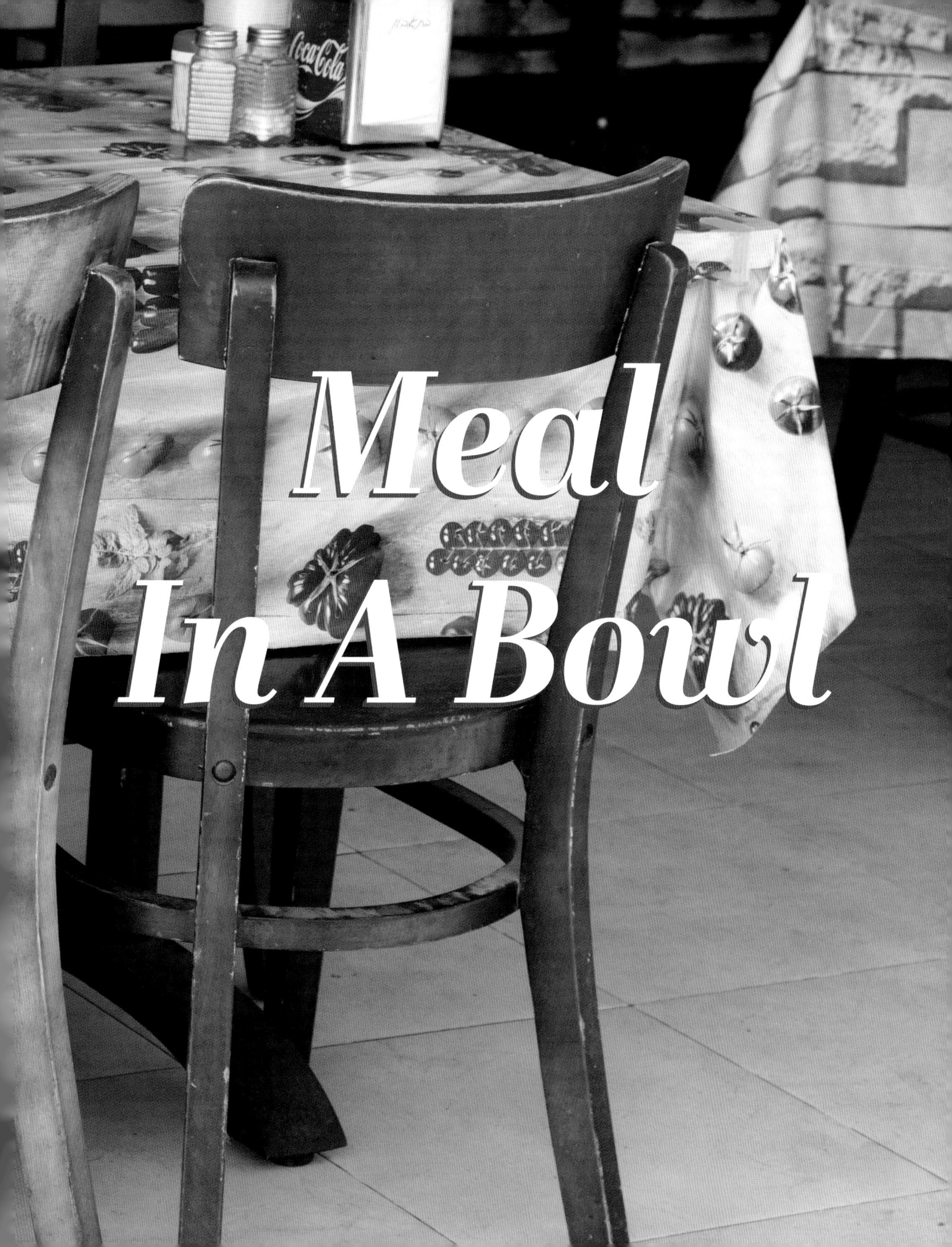

Meal In A Bowl

MY MUM SHULAMIT

My mother is my main culinary inspiration. To this day I consult with her about cooking on a daily basis. Now I appreciate it but when you're a kid, you take home cooking for granted.

One day my friend at primary school asked me to play at her home after school. 'Don't worry, we can eat at my place,' she said. I got my mum's permission to visit as my friend lived 5 minutes away from school. I was curious to see what would be on the menu. We were sitting in the kitchen while her mother prepared the food. She opened a can of meatloaf, sliced it, pan-fried it and served it with a bottle of red sauce called ketchup! I had never tasted ketchup before and I was instantly addicted to that sweet tomato flavour. I rushed home, excited to tell my mum about the new sauce. I asked her, 'Please make it with that meatloaf, it was so good!' My poor mum, who never made us food out of a can, reluctantly cooked it for me.

My mum began to cook when she was eight years old. As the oldest girl, she looked after the siblings when her mother was sick in hospital. One day she had to make a lentil soup to serve six people. It was the first time she had made such a soup. In her inexperience, she measured out six soup bowls of lentils, one bowl for each person instead of two cups in total. When the soup came to the boil, the lentils burst out of the pan in a dreadful mess. She was upset, worried about what her father would say — but he just laughed! Learning to cook at such a young age was a tough experience, but that's what made my mum into the cook she is today.

My mother cooked fresh food for us every day. At school I looked forward to seeing which sandwich I had that morning: salami with pickles, egg mayonnaise, avocado, cheese and tomato or chopped olives mixed with margarine (a particular delight). My favourite sandwich was made with Hashahar's chocolate spread, which I still consider the best chocolate spread in the world.

Her care for and devotion to us affected me profoundly. I remember coming home from school on a rainy winter's day, soaked to the bone. Immediately mum changed my clothes, dressed me in warm pyjamas, sat me next to the heater and fed me some hearty soup that warmed my body and raised my spirit.

She was there for us, no matter whether she was ill or tired. If she had to stay in hospital for a few days after giving birth, she used to sneak out for a couple of hours a day to come home and cook for us. She was, and is, an old-fashioned mum. A 24-hours-a-day mother, always looking after her children.

MY DAD YOAV

My dad grew up during the 1950s in Tel Aviv to the sound of rock and roll, when Elvis Presley was the King. He loved Elvis so much that he used to dress like him. If you wanted to see Elvis you just had to look at my dad. I remember how, as a little girl, I used to blow-dry my dad's hair with great care to give him the trademark Elvis quiff.

Dad has always been a fantastic dancer and he still is: rock and roll, twist and swing. Whenever he dances, he smiles as if he's in a happy dream. We had a record player in our sitting room. My dad used to call me in to listen to the old songs and check to see if I knew the names of the songs and performers. By the age of seven I was familiar with the legendary music of Elvis, Brenda Lee, Dean Martin, Ray Charles, Patsy Cline, Paul Anka, Johnny Cash, Frank Sinatra and more. Today when I cook, I listen to the timeless music of the '50s and '60s and think of my dad and all the wonderful times we have shared.

My dad didn't have much growing up. He worked hard to provide his children with everything he had missed out on. We played hide and seek together when he returned from work in the afternoons. Every week he bought us Belgian chocolates — the most delicious I have ever tasted — from a tiny shop in King George Street. My dad has always been what we would nowadays call a foodie. Whenever a new eating place opened in Tel Aviv, my father scooped us up and took us there to try the food.

Dad is a real gentleman. He taught us to think about others and to be generous. Every year before my mother's birthday, as I was the oldest child, he used to take me with him to buy her a gift. When he returns from a shopping trip, he brings back something extra for my mum, a special treat just for her.

My father grew up in a neighbourhood next to Jaffa so he became fluent in Arabic. His friends included Arabic Muslims and Christians. Once a week as a family we used to sit together and watch an Arabic film on TV. Sometimes dad would take us to visit his Arabic friends in Jaffa which is how I became smitten with Arabic food. They would serve us home-made hummus and broad bean falafels, crispy outside, melting in the middle and with a distinctive earthy flavour. On one of my visits I went to play outside their house with their son, who was two years younger than me. I wanted to talk to him so I said the first words that came to my mind: 'Ana Mehibek'. The boy looked at me then ran straight back to his mum. 'Ana Mehibek' means 'I love you!'

In those days, our TV was black and white, a huge box with an indoor antenna that stood on top of the set. My dad used to watch the news in the evenings and the sport on Thursday nights. Unfortunately for me, when the reception was bad, my dad would call me in to hold the antenna. 'Hold it.... A little bit higher... That's it! Now don't move.' Sometimes I found myself holding the antenna for an hour!

FASULYA

SERVES 6–8

- 500g (1lb 2oz) haricot beans, soaked overnight
- 800g (1lb 12oz) boneless shin of beef, cut into 2cm (¾in) cubes
- 3 pieces of marrow bone
- 5 garlic cloves, chopped
- 1 tbsp olive oil

FLAVOURING

- 2–3 tbsp sugar
- Salt and pepper
- ½ tbsp paprika
- 4–5 tbsp tomato paste
- 1 tsp ground cumin
- 1 tsp crushed coriander seeds (optional)
- A generous handful of chopped coriander
- 1 tbsp chicken stock powder
- 250ml (1 cup) boiling water
- 400g (14oz) can of chopped tomatoes (optional)
- Chilli flakes, to taste (optional)

TIP: I like to substitute 200g (7oz) of cubed lamb shoulder for the same weight of beef shin for extra flavour. I usually use haricot beans as they're smaller and cook faster, but you can use other white beans instead.

Drain the soaked beans and put them in a large, deep saucepan with the meat and marrow bones. Cover generously with cold water and bring to the boil over a high heat. As soon as it begins to boil, thoroughly skim off any scum, then add the garlic and olive oil. Return to the boil, then reduce heat and simmer, covered, for an hour. Test by taking out a bean and pressing it with a fork. If it mashes easily, the beans are soft enough, if not cook for a further 20 minutes.

Mix all the flavouring ingredients and add to the soup. Bring to the boil, reduce the heat and cook, covered, for 30 minutes. Uncover and cook for 10 minutes over medium-high heat to reduce slightly. Taste and adjust the seasoning as required.

Serve with white rice.

This substantial soup is a dish my mother cooked for us on rainy winter days. There are versions of it in many Mediterranean countries and it's a popular street food in Tel Aviv. This recipe is my mother's special version — it's very simple to make as the meat is simmered rather than fried, while the garlic and coriander give it a real depth of flavour.

MY PERFECT CHICKEN SOUP

MAKES AROUND 5–6 LITRES (AROUND 5–6 QUARTS)

2 chicken legs, skinless
12 chicken wings, cleaned
8 chicken necks or 2 chicken carcasses
3 carrots, peeled
1 onion, peeled
2 leeks, white part only
2 celery stalks
2–3 garlic cloves, peeled
1 potato, peeled
1 parsnip, peeled
1 courgette (zucchini) (optional)
75g (3½ oz) fresh dill
40g (1½ oz) fresh parsley
Sea salt

TO SERVE
Short vermicelli (lokshen)
Sor mandel (Israeli mini soup croutons)

Place the chicken pieces in a large pot. Cover with cold water and bring to the boil. Drain the pieces, discarding the water, so as to get rid of any impurities and excess fat.

Rinse the chicken well in cold water and return to the pot. Add 6 litres (6 quarts) of water, cover and simmer gently over low heat for an hour. Add the remaining ingredients and season with salt; cover and simmer for a further hour.

Strain the stock, setting aside the chicken pieces and vegetables. From these, reserve only the chicken legs and necks, the carrots, potato, and courgette (zucchini); discard the remainder.

Pass the stock through a muslin-lined sieve. Return it to the pan, cover and simmer gently for 3 hours more. This extra simmering gives the stock a richness of colour and adds a wonderful depth of flavour. Add the reserved chicken and vegetables to the stock and simmer gently until heated through.

Serve the soup with short vermicelli (lokshen) and sor mandel (Israeli mini soup croutons). For special occasions, we eat it with Kreplach (see p.239).

There's a golden rule for making soups, which is to first cook the ingredient you want your soup to taste of. That's why I simmer the chicken first for an hour, then add the vegetables. The result is a chicken soup that really tastes of chicken — try my recipe and you'll see for yourself. The flavour of the soup is the comforting taste of childhood. This beautiful healthy soup, as all grandmothers and mothers know, is an excellent remedy for colds and flu — guaranteed!

MUM'S SWEET AND SOUR CABBAGE SOUP

SERVES 8

SOUP
4 tbsp oil
1 large onion, chopped
½ white cabbage, chopped
1 cup of sauerkraut (drained)
3 litres (12 cups) chicken stock
5 tbsp tomato paste
Juice of 1 lemon
Salt and black pepper
1–2 tbsp vinegar
3–4 tbsp sugar
2 bay leaves
100g (½ cup) white rice

MEATBALLS (OPTIONAL)
500g minced beef or chicken
1 large onion, chopped and fried in a little oil until golden brown
1 egg
2 tbsp matzo meal
Salt and pepper

Heat the oil in a saucepan over medium heat. Add the onion and fry until translucent. Add the cabbage, reduce the heat, cover and cook for 30 minutes, stirring now and then, until the cabbage is softened.

Add all the remaining soup ingredients apart from the rice. Bring to the boil, then taste and adjust seasoning – the soup should be sweet and sour. Cover and cook over a low heat for 1 hour. Add the rice and cook for 10 minutes till soft. If it's too thick for your taste, thin with boiling water. Serve at once.

To make with meatballs, mix together the beef, fried onion, egg and matzo meal. Season with salt and pepper. Shape into ping pong ball-sized meatballs. Add to the cabbage when you add the stock and other ingredients.

My mother has fond memories of this traditional Ashkenazi soup, which she first ate at primary school. When I came to London, I came across the soup because my Ashkenazi neighbours made it. I liked it so much that I cooked it myself. My mother was here on a visit and when she ate it, she said: 'This is the soup I had at school – and you've cooked it perfectly!'

VELVET CAULIFLOWER SOUP

SERVES 6

- 4 tbsp olive oil
- 1 onion, finely chopped
- 1kg (2lb 4oz) cauliflower florets (fresh or frozen and defrosted)
- 2 potatoes, cubed
- 750ml (3 cups) chicken stock
- 4 tbsp white wine
- 1 tsp sugar
- Salt and pepper
- Pinch of grated nutmeg
- 125ml (½ cup) whipping cream
- 25g (2 tbsp) butter
- 1 garlic clove, crushed
- A little parsley, chopped

Heat the olive oil in a saucepan and fry the onion till golden. Add the cauliflower, reserving 100g (3½ oz) of the florets for garnish, and the potato, stock, wine and sugar. Season with salt and pepper and nutmeg. Stir and bring to the boil. Reduce the heat, cover and simmer over a low heat for 20 minutes, until the vegetables are soft.

Blend the soup with a hand blender till creamy and smooth. Add the cream and bring to the boil. Stir well and remove from the heat.

Melt the butter in a small pan. Roughly chop the reserved cauliflower and fry till golden. Add the crushed garlic, mixing with the cauliflower, and remove from the heat at once. Divide the soup into serving dishes and garnish each portion with the fried cauliflower and a sprinkling of chopped parsley.

"A smooth, velvety soup, perfect warming food for a winter's day."

BROAD BEAN AND BONE MARROW SOUP

SERVES 6

800g (1lb 12oz) frozen baby broad beans, defrosted
3–4 tbsp oil
1 onion, finely chopped
2 celery stalks, strings peeled off and very finely chopped
6 pieces marrow bone, with marrow intact
2 litre (8 cups) chicken stock
2 potatoes, peeled and cubed
Juice and finely grated zest of 1 lemon
1 tsp sugar (optional)
Salt and white pepper
Handful of celery leaves (optional)
Sliced baguette, to serve

Double-pod the beans (if needed), popping them out of their tough skins.

Heat the oil in a large saucepan. Over a medium heat, fry the onion and celery until just golden. Add in the broad beans, marrow bones and stock. Bring to the boil, skim, add the potatoes, lemon juice and zest. Season with sugar, salt and white pepper and add the celery leaves if using. Bring to the boil, reduce the heat, cover and simmer for 30–40 minutes more. Stir the soup, taste it and adjust the seasoning as required. Serve with bread.

Even though it looks rustic, this is truly a gourmet soup. It is a dish my Moroccan grandmother used to make for Passover and I always loved it. Spread the bone marrow on a slice of baguette and eat it with a spoonful of soup — the combination is amazing!

EASY TOMATO SOUP

SERVES 4–6

4 tbsp olive oil
30g (2 tbsp) butter
2–3 onions, quartered
10 ripe plum tomatoes
3 garlic cloves, sliced
1 large celery stalk, strings peeled off, roughly chopped
1 litre (4 cups) hot vegetable stock
Salt and pepper
1–2 sprigs of basil
100g (3½ oz) small soup pasta

Handful of chopped celery leaves, to serve
Grated Parmesan, to serve

Heat olive oil and butter in a saucepan. Add the onion, tomatoes, garlic and celery, cover and cook over a very low heat for 45–60 minutes, shaking the saucepan now and then, so the vegetables stew in their own juices.

Using a hand blender, chop the cooked vegetables in the saucepan. Pass them through a sieve and return the sieved ingredients to the pan. Add the stock, mix, and bring to the boil. Season with salt and pepper, add the basil sprigs and pasta, and cook for 10 minutes over medium heat, until the pasta is cooked through. Discard the basil. Serve garnished with celery leaves, and with Parmesan on the side.

There is very little chopping required for this soup, so it really is easy to make. Allowing the vegetables to stew in their own juices gives a great depth of flavour and the result is a delicious and colourful soup.

YOELI'S VEGETABLE BARLEY SOUP

SERVES 8

3 tbsp oil
1 onion, finely chopped
2 carrots, peeled and cubed
700g (1lb 9oz) sweet potatoes, peeled and cubed
1 potato, peeled and cubed
100g (3½ oz) pearl barley
1.25 litres (5 cups) chicken or vegetable stock
1 tomato, cubed
1 courgette (zucchini), cubed
1 bay leaf
Salt and pepper
1 tsp sugar

Heat the oil in a saucepan over a medium heat and fry the onion, stirring now and then, for around 10 minutes, until golden. Add all the remaining ingredients and bring to the boil. Cover and cook over a low heat for 45 minutes, until the vegetables have softened. Taste and adjust the seasoning as required.

Variation:
For a thick and creamy soup, remove 500ml (2 cups) of the cooked soup to another container and blend until smooth using a hand blender. Return to the saucepan and mix in.

This is my son Yoeli's favourite soup. On cold winter days, I like to make it as a warming surprise for when he comes home from school.

12
12
12
12
12
10
10
1.0
1.0

HEARTY RED LENTIL SOUP

SERVES 5–6

2 tbsp olive oil
30g (2 tbsp) butter
1 small onion, chopped
3–4 garlic cloves, chopped
1 tsp sweet paprika or turmeric
200g (7oz) red lentils, rinsed
500ml (2 cups) hot chicken or vegetable stock
1–2 tsp sugar
Salt and pepper
60g (2oz) short vermicelli (lokshen)
Handful of chopped coriander
Juice of ½ lemon

Heat the oil and butter in a saucepan over medium-low heat. Add the onion and fry for 10 minutes, stirring now and then, until lightly golden. Add garlic and paprika. Mix and fry for 1 minute.

Add the lentils and enough water to cover by 2.5cm (1in). Cover, bring to the boil, reduce heat and simmer for 20 minutes until the lentils are soft.

Add the stock and season with sugar, salt and pepper. Mix together, bring to the boil, and add the vermicelli and the coriander. Cover and simmer over a low heat for 3–5 minutes. Add the lemon juice, mixing it in. Taste and adjust the seasoning.

This soup really is a meal in a bowl! The lentils and noodles make it very satisfying. It was my mother's favourite soup when she was a child. I cook it every week for my boys to brighten up the day.

ש.מ שיווק הדרים
פרי הדר
ירקות ופירות מעולים זה...
Givememore

Delicious Dips & Rainbow Salads

HUMMUS

MAKES AROUND 1 KILO

300g (1½ cups) small dried chickpeas, pre-soaked (see method)
2 tsp bicarbonate of soda
100ml (3½ fl oz) cup tahini paste
Juice of 1–2 lemons
2 garlic cloves, chopped
Salt

TO GARNISH
Olive oil
50g (2 oz) reserved chickpeas
Sweet paprika
Ground cumin
Chopped parsley

Soak the chickpeas in plenty of cold water with 1 tsp bicarbonate of soda for 20 hours. Drain the soaked chickpeas and rinse them well; at this stage, if not using at once, you can freeze them.

Place the chickpeas in a large saucepan and cover generously with water to around 15cm/6in above the level of the chickpeas. Bring to the boil, then reduce heat, cover and simmer for 1½ hours. Remove around 200ml (7 fl oz) of the cooking water and set aside to cool.

Add 1 tsp bicarbonate of soda to the chickpeas (bearing in mind that it will froth up). Cook for a further hour, until the chickpeas are so soft that you can mash them between your fingers. Drain, but don't rinse them. Reserve around 50g (2 oz) of the chickpeas to use as a garnish.

Place the chickpeas, tahini, and a third of the reserved cooking water in a food processor, and process until smooth. If too thick for your taste, add more of the cooking water. Add half the lemon juice, process and taste, adding more lemon juice if needed. Add the garlic and salt to taste, and process until smooth. Once made, store it in the fridge where it keeps for 5 days.

To serve, place a portion in a shallow serving dish. Swirl with a spoon to create a hollow in the centre. Pour in olive oil, then top with the reserved chickpeas, sweet paprika, ground cumin and parsley. Serve with Zhoug (see p.70) on the side and Za'atar Pitta (see p.387).

Hummus is Israel's national dish — so important in Israel that practically every home in the country will have a tub of it in the fridge. There are food shops called Humusia that specialise in hummus, offering it with a range of toppings such as warm mushrooms, pieces of grilled lamb or falafel. Hummus together with foul and tahini is the Holy Trinity of Israeli cuisine.

Home-made hummus is a great, nutritious food to make. Be sure to use small chickpeas as these have the best flavour. For once, smaller is better!

ZHOUG

MAKES AROUND 450G (1LB)

15 long green chillies (mild ones)
3 red chillies (hot ones)
2–3 green chillies (hot ones)
1 large bunch of coriander (cilantro)
12–13 garlic cloves
1 tsp salt
1–2 tsp ground cumin
Pinch of cardamom powder
2 tbsp oil
1 tbsp white vinegar or white wine vinegar

TIP: I use a mixture of mild and hot chillies, so as to get a good level of both heat and chilli flavour. If you find the zhoug too hot for your palate, squeeze fresh lemon juice over it to tone down the heat.

De-seed the chillies, scraping out the seeds and the white pith, then roughly chop. Cut the coriander just below the leaves, use the leafy part (including stalks). Place the chillies, garlic and coriander in a food processor and process until finely chopped.

Add the salt, cumin and cardamom powder and blend again. Taste to check the seasoning. Mix in the oil and vinegar.

Serve at once or store covered in the fridge for a week. I like to portion it up into small tubs and freeze it so I always have some on hand.

Serving suggestion: Grate 1–2 tomatoes and mix with 1–2 tsp zhoug.

"If you don't make it hot, you don't make zhoug!"

Zhoug, originally Yemenite, has become an indispensable part of Israeli cuisine. In Israel it's served as a condiment with street food like Falafel, Sabich and Shawarma (see Taste of Tel Aviv for recipes), adding a great chilli kick. When you serve Hummus (see p.68) it's essential. A good Zhoug is always chilli-hot – traditionally the women who made it would compete to see who could make the hottest! There is a red Zhoug, made from dried chillies, but I prefer green zhoug, fragrant with herbs and spices. It used to be made with a pestle and mortar, but nowadays, thanks to the magic of food processors, it's very quick and easy to make. I always have zhoug in my fridge to feed my sons' chilli habit!

CHARRED AUBERGINE (EGGPLANT) DIP

SERVES 5–6

3 aubergines (eggplant)
3 garlic cloves, crushed
1 tbsp mayonnaise
Salt and pepper

TIP: choose smooth, unblemished aubergines (eggplant) which are light in weight.

Char the aubergines (eggplant) Place a metal grill on the hob (cooktop) and put the aubergines on the rack. Cook over a high heat until charred on all sides, taking care not to pierce their skins as you turn them, until they are softened and thoroughly blackened. If you don't have gas, use your grill (broiler) to cook the vegetables in the same way.

Transfer the cooked aubergines (eggplant) to a plate and set aside to cool. Carefully peel off the charred skin, rinse them under a tap and trim off the stem, placing the flesh in a sieve over a bowl. Alternately, cut off each stalk, slice lengthways and scoop out pulp into a sieve over a bowl. With your hands, squeeze out the excess moisture.

Place the aubergine flesh, garlic and mayonnaise in a bowl; season with salt and pepper. Using a fork, mix vigorously until well blended. If you want a smoother texture briefly use a hand blender.

If you walk past a block of flats in Israel on a Thursday afternoon or Friday morning, the air is bound to smell of aubergines (eggplant) being charred in preparation for Shabbat. Cooking them in this way imparts a delicious smoky aroma and flavour. My mother used to make this for us most weeks and I would enjoy eating it warm or at room temperature, mopped up with bread.

MOROCCAN MATBUKHA

7–8 tbsp oil
5–6 long, mild, light green peppers, finely sliced
6–7 hot chillies (red or green), finely sliced
1 head of garlic, cloves peeled and finely chopped
1 tbsp sweet paprika
13–15 ripe tomatoes, scalded, skinned and chopped
1 level tbsp salt
1 tbsp sugar

Heat 4 tbsp oil in a frying pan over medium heat. Add the green peppers and the chillies and fry, stirring, until they begin to soften (around 2–3 minutes). Add the garlic and fry for 1 minute, stirring. Mix in the paprika and fry, stirring, for 30 seconds. Remove from heat.

Place the tomatoes in a wide, heavy-based saucepan, add the contents of the frying pan and mix together. Cook over a medium-low heat for around 1–2 hours, stirring often with a wooden spoon to prevent it burning until most of the liquid from the vegetables has evaporated.

Season with salt and cook, stirring constantly, for up to 10 minutes to cook off the residual water. Add the sugar and stir. Taste and adjust the seasoning. You want nearly all the water to have cooked off, with only oily bubbles remaining. Add the remaining oil and stir; the mixture should be glossy.

Cool and store in a covered container in a fridge for up to 10 days.

I serve matbukha with fresh Challah (see p.183) as part of the Shabbat table.

Other serving suggestions:

- For a quick guacamole, add 2 tbsp of matbukha to chopped or mashed avocados.
- For an easy shakshuka, use the matbukha as a ready-made base.
- Use it as a spicy sandwich spread or add to sauces.

A definitive Moroccan matbukha recipe is hard to find, as everyone has their own secret recipe with their own touch or mixture of ingredients. This recipe is one I pieced together over the years from recipes given to me by family and friends and found in books. I fry the chillies and garlic first in order to bring out their flavour. A good matbukha should be glossy and have a texture like jam, with no liquid in it. It is a wonderful, versatile food, but I like it best eaten straight with bread.

TZATZIKI

SERVES 4–5

3 cucumbers, peeled, coarsely grated, and squeezed dry
500g (1lb 2oz) Greek yogurt
1–2 garlic cloves, crushed
1 tbsp chopped dill or 1 tsp dried mint
½ tbsp white wine vinegar
Salt
Olive oil, to drizzle

TIP: If you can't get Greek yogurt, use a 50/50 mixture of yogurt and sour cream.

Mix together the cucumber, yogurt, garlic, dill and vinegar. Season with salt, drizzle with olive oil and serve.

In the warm, sunny Middle East, we enjoy eating refreshing cucumber and yogurt dishes, like the chilled soup my mother used to make. You find this combination of ingredients all over the Balkans and the Mediterranean. In Greece, it is a thick, creamy-textured dip, whereas the Syrians thin the yogurt with water and serve it as a soup. I like this Greek version, which I often serve with Courgette (zucchini) Fritters (p.139), Latkes (p.125) or Stuffed Vine Leaves (p.243).

MIAMI HEAT
CHELSEA
MARYLAND
PEPSI
SALE!!

Vex

TOUM

MAKES AROUND 1–1.5 LITRES (4–6 CUPS)

- 3 large heads of garlic at room temperature, cloves peeled
- 1 tsp salt
- 1 litre (4 cups) sunflower oil
- Juice of 1 lemon, at room temperature

Make sure your food processor is totally dry. Add the garlic cloves and sprinkle over the salt. Pulse for 20 seconds, then scrape down the garlic from the sides. Repeat the pulsing and scraping down process 3 times, until the garlic turns into a thick, smooth paste.

With the machine now running constantly, add a slender stream of around 100ml (3½ fl oz) of oil very gradually so it becomes incorporated with the garlic. Blend for 10 seconds more. Add 1 tsp lemon juice and blend for 10 seconds until well absorbed.

Now add ½ tsp lemon juice, blending well, then very gradually add in 125ml (½ cup) oil in a slender stream and blend for 10 seconds, so that the mixture emulsifies.

Repeat this process of gradually adding the lemon juice and oil alternately. By the end of it, the toum should be white and thick, resembling whipped yogurt. Do not rush this process or the toum will split; it should take around 8–10 minutes.

If the mixture begins to curdle, you can discard the curdled part and use what remains. If it all curdles, then you will have to throw it all away and start again.

When the toum has just been made, it will be warm from the blending process. Transfer it to a container without stirring or covering and set aside to cool thoroughly. Be sure to skim off any moisture that forms on the surface before covering and refrigerating. It will keep in the fridge for up to a month. While the toum is stored in the fridge, however, open up the container every few days and wipe off any condensation that has formed on the inside of the lid. It's important that it remain dry as otherwise the texture will be spoiled.

Ta-da — let me introduce you to toum! This bright white, light-textured garlic dip is found in London's best Lebanese restaurants — a wonderful accompaniment to grilled meat. I simply don't understand why toum hasn't yet found its way to Israel. Once I tasted it, I knew it would go well with chicken shashlik. Stored properly, it will keep for a month in the fridge and is a useful substitute for fresh garlic in dishes such as meatballs or fish balls or for brushing grilled chicken. Toum's one disadvantage? It keeps people at a distance!

OLIVIER – RUSSIAN POTATO SALAD

SERVES 5–6

1kg (2¼lb) small salad potatoes
2 large carrots, peeled
3 eggs, hard-boiled, peeled and diced
2–3 gherkins, diced
100g (½ cup) cooked peas
4–5 tbsp mayonnaise (or substitute 2 tbsp sour cream for 2 tbsp mayonnaise)
Salt and pepper
1 tsp smooth mustard (optional)
2 tbsp chopped dill (optional)

Boil the potatoes and carrots until tender: drain. While they are still warm, peel and cube the potatoes and cube the carrots.

Mix the potato and carrot with the remaining ingredients at once, seasoning with salt and pepper. Serve at room temperature or chilled.

Whenever I see this salad I'm transported back to my childhood home by the sea in Tel Aviv. Every Friday, I would watch my Mum make Olivier salad. It is especially tasty when freshly made and eaten while still warm. By the time she got it into the fridge, half of it would have vanished!

ISRAELI SALAD

SERVES 4

- **3 thin, firm, small (Lebanese) cucumbers, finely diced**
- **2 ripe but firm tomatoes, finely diced**
- **½ red onion or 4 spring onions/scallions, finely chopped**
- **A handful of parsley leaves**
- **Juice of ½ lemon**
- **2 tbsp oil**
- **Salt and pepper**

TIP: For a Syrian version, add ½ tsp ground cumin.

Gently mix all the ingredients together, seasoning with salt. Serve at once.

In Israel this popular salad, also known as Arabic Salad, is enjoyed throughout the day. It is a simple local recipe, an expression of the abundance of our vegetables and the richness of the soil. Make sure that the cucumbers and tomatoes you use are fresh and firm. As a little girl, I always used to drink the juice from the salad left in the bowl. In fact, to this day, I still do that — but don't tell anyone!

מסגרית הכפר
03-9320139
משלוחים חינם
מכבדים כרטיסי אשראי
תפוזים רשת 6.90
כרוב 5.90
אשכולית אדומה 8.90
בצל יבש 5.90
מבצע! תפוחים א.א. 10.90
מבצע! תפוחים א.א. 10.90
מבצע תפוחים א.א. 10.90
מבצע תפוזים 6.90
קלמנטינה דבש 9.80
תפוחים 4.90
מבצע תפוחים 10.90
מבצע תפוחים 10.90

קלמנטינה
9.80
תפוחים מובחרים
10.90
כרובית
6.90
פומלה
9.90
מבצע כרובית
6.90
מבצע פומלה
9.90
מבצע כרובית
6.90
מבצע פומלה
9.90
תירס סיוון מעולה
אבוקדו בשל לאכילה

COLESLAW

SERVES 8

½ large white cabbage*, shredded
3 large carrots, coarsely grated

*Choose a large white cabbage, as large cabbages are sweeter. Small cabbages are usually bitter.

OPTIONAL ADDITIONS FOR A RICHER COLESLAW

3–4 spring onions/scallions, chopped
A handful of chopped parsley

FOR A PINK COLESLAW

Adding a large handful of shredded red cabbage to the mixture gives a pretty pinkish tinge to the coleslaw.

DRESSING

4 tbsp mayonnaise (or substitute 2 tbsp sour cream for 2 tbsp mayonnaise)
1 heaped tsp smooth mustard
1–2 tbsp sugar
Salt and pepper
2–3 tbsp lemon juice or vinegar
2–3 tbsp water

Place the cabbage and carrots in a large bowl. Mix the dressing ingredients, preferably using a hand blender, and pour into the bowl. Using your hands, thoroughly mix until the cabbage and carrot are well coated. Serve at once or store in the fridge in an airtight container.

In Jewish cuisine coleslaw is a fundamental food. We eat it with everything — add it to sandwiches, eat it in pitta and in hamburgers, enjoy it with grilled chicken, schnitzel or barbecued meat. It really is *the* Jewish Salad!

EGG SALAD

SERVES 8

6 hard-boiled eggs, peeled
4–5 spring onions/scallions, green part only, sliced
2 tbsp chopped dill
2–3 tbsp mayonnaise
1–2 tsp smooth mustard
Salt and pepper

Mash the eggs using a potato masher or a fork, or chop. Add the remaining ingredients and mix well.

This my children's favourite sandwich filling, topped with a layer of cress. We also enjoy it eating it with chopped liver on Shabbat.

MOROCCAN BEETROOT SALAD

SERVES 6

- 4 large raw beetroot/beets
- Salt
- 2–3 tbsp sugar
- Juice of 1–2 lemons
- 1 celery stalk, tough strings peeled and finely chopped (optional)

GARNISH

- Chopped beetroot/beet leaves or parsley

Place the beetroot/beets in a saucepan, cover generously with cold water and bring to the boil. Reduce the heat, cover and simmer for 1½ to 2 hours, until tender. Drain and cool, then peel and chop into 2.5cm/1in cubes

Before seasoning, taste the beetroot/beets. If it tastes sweet, use only 2 tbsp sugar; if it's not sweet, add more sugar. Season the cubes with salt, sugar and lemon juice, mixing well.

Garnish with leaves and serve.

This healthy salad is one that my late grandmother used to make for me. With its beautiful colour and sweet flavour it's a salad that children love.

TURKISH SALAD

SERVES 7–8

- 10 spring onions/scallions, finely chopped
- A handful of chopped flat leaf parsley
- 2 tbsp good harissa (I like 'Harry' brand)
- 1 heaped tbsp tomato paste
- 5 tbsp oil
- 3 tbsp fresh lemon juice
- ½ tbsp ground cumin
- 1 tsp sugar

Mix all ingredients together. Taste and adjust the lemon juice and sugar levels as required. (As harissa is so salty, I don't use salt.) Serve with hummus and pitta or spread in sandwiches.

This piquant Turkish salad is very popular in Israel, sold in every supermarket and grocery store. I'd always bought it ready-made, but one day my Mum rang me to say she'd made it herself and that it tasted 'better than the supermarket version'. She gave me the recipe and was right — freshly made, free from preservatives, the taste is amazing.

QUINOA SALAD

SERVES 4

- 200g (1 cup) quinoa (I like to use a mixture of red and white quinoa)
- 1 tsp salt
- Pomegranate seeds from 1 pomegranate
- 4 spring onions/scallions, green part only, sliced
- A handful of finely chopped parsley
- A handful of dried cranberries
- A generous handful of fresh rocket
- 3 tbsp pomegranate molasses
- 1 tbsp olive oil

Rinse quinoa in sieve to remove any grit.

Place the quinoa in a saucepan, cover well with water and add 1 tsp salt. Bring to the boil and cook over medium high until quinoa is softened and translucent. Drain and set aside to dry,

Place the quinoa in a serving bowl. Add in the remaining ingredients and mix well. Serve immediately or cover and chill until required.

> "I was not a quinoa fan. My Mum, keen to get me to eat this healthy food, created this colourful salad for me. It's now a firm favourite."

LEEK AND TOMATO SALAD

SERVES 6–8

3–4 slender leeks
300g (10oz) cherry tomatoes, halved
6–7 baby sweetcorn, sliced
2 tbsp mayonnaise
1–2 tsp mustard
Salt and pepper

TIP: Add a handful of chopped coriander for extra flavour.

Remove the tough outer layer from the leeks. Trim off the root end and the green part. Slice the leeks lengthways, and then cut across finely into slices 5mm (around ¼ in) thick.

Place the leeks, cherry tomatoes and sweetcorn in a serving bowl.

Mix the mayonnaise with the mustard. Add the mayonnaise mixture to the leek mixture. Gently mix together until well coated. Season with salt and pepper. Serve.

I first came across this salad at a catering stall. I liked it so much that I asked them for the recipe. They kindly shared it with me, and now it's part of my salad repertoire!

CUCUMBER RADISH SALAD

SERVES 4–6

6 large crisp lettuce leaves, such as iceberg or romaine
2–3 cucumbers
2–3 tbsp chopped dill leaves
4 radishes, finely sliced
¼ red onion, finely chopped

DRESSING

Generous 5 tbsp olive oil
1 garlic clove, crushed
1 heaped tsp mayonnaise
Pinch of coarse salt
Juice of ½–1 lemon
1 tbsp red wine vinegar
1 tsp balsamic vinegar
1–2 tsp honey
1 tsp za'atar

Slice off and discard the stem-end of the lettuce leaves. Shred the trimmed lettuce leaves. Halve the cucumbers lengthways and scoop out the seeds. Slice.

Whisk together the dressing ingredients. Taste to check the seasoning and adjust to taste.

Toss together the lettuce, cucumber, dill, radishes and onion. Toss the salad with the dressing. Serve at once.

This crunchy and refreshing salad is excellent served with fried fish.

My Home By The Sea

Jaffa, Old City

BEAUTIFUL SUMMER WEEKENDS

On hot summer Fridays, straight after school, my father used to take us to the beach around the corner from our home. The beach was quiet, with shallow rock pools which I would sit in and look for tiny crabs. I would put them in my bucket and sit on the rocks under the sun to warm up.

I remember the ice lolly (ice pop) man who used to pass through the beach with his shouts of: 'Eskimo, Eskimo! Lemon! Banana, chocolate, vanilla!' It sounded like music to me. My dear dad would buy us all lollies.

We felt famished after we played on the beach. My thoughtful mum provided us with supplies: warm pittas filled with meatballs and soft potatoes in tomato sauce, which soaked through the pitta. What a tasty snack. I would sit on a deck chair, huddled in my towel, relishing every bite while facing the endless sea.

My father would take us around town on the weekend. Tel Aviv in the 1970s was the place for a child to be! We went to the Tel Aviv Zoo, the funfair, Jaffa, Dizengoff Street with its trendy cafés and happening cultural scene and the grand beach in front of the Sheraton Hotel. Those trips always included new tastes and experiences. For breakfast he would take us to Jerusalem Street in Jaffa, where we ate at the legendary Burekas Sami and devoured mastic ice cream. At the port of Jaffa we lunched on freshly grilled *barbunya* (red mullet). It was cooked to perfection: crispy pink skin on the outside, succulent white flesh inside.

I remember when I tasted my first American ice cream in a small ice cream shop on Dizengoff Street. I was fascinated by the ice cream machine, the variety of toppings and the fluffy whipped cream on top. By the time I'd eaten the whipped cream and toppings I was too full to eat the ice cream. Whenever we went for an American ice cream from then on, my father bought me just whipped cream and toppings! On the Sheraton Hotel beach, we would enjoy their beloved Snow Ice Cream and sometimes on our way home we would stop for the original Malabi (Middle Eastern milk pudding).

PICKLED HERRINGS

MAKES 12 BISMARCK HERRING FILLETS

12 fresh, salted skinless Bismarck herring fillets
Dill sprigs, to garnish (optional)

MARINADE
3 large onions
13 allspice berries
6 dried bay leaves
300ml (1¼ cup) white vinegar
250ml (1 cup) water
2–3 tbsp sugar

TIP: Pre-salted Bismarck herring fillets for pickling can be bought from kosher fish shops.

Make the marinade. Peel the onions and halve lengthways. Slice finely across into semicircles.

Place all the marinade ingredients in a pot. Bring just to boiling point, taste and adjust the flavour as required. Remove the marinade from direct heat and set aside to stand until completely cool.

Cut each herring fillet into pieces, roughly 4cm (1½ in) square.

Take a large sterilized preserving jar with a capacity of 1 litre (4 cups). Layer a generous spoonful of the onion mixture in the bottom followed by a few pieces of herring. Repeat this alternate layering until the jar is four-fifths full. Now pour in the marinade to fill the jar. It is important to cover the herring thoroughly. Close the jar and refrigerate overnight to marinate.

Once made, these can be eaten the following day. They can be stored in the fridge for 2–3 weeks. Serve garnished with dill sprigs accompanied by bread.

“When I was a child, my mother used to make these for the family. My brother and I would wait impatiently by the fridge, asking her every half an hour: ‘Are they ready yet?’

39474
70954

SALMON IN SPINACH CREAM SAUCE

SERVES 4

4 x skinless salmon fillets, each 200g (7oz)
Salt and coarsely ground black pepper
30g (2 tbsp) butter

SAUCE
70g (4½ tbsp) butter
800g (1lb 12oz) fresh spinach
125ml (½ cup) white wine
Ground black pepper
350ml (1½ cups) double (heavy) cream
1 tbsp Dijon mustard
Grated zest of ½ lemon (optional)

GARNISH
3–4 tbsp chopped chives

Cook the salmon: Season the salmon fillets on both sides with salt and pepper. Heat the butter in a wide frying pan over medium heat until frothing, add fish and fry 3 minutes on each side. Carefully remove from the pan and keep warm.

Sauce: Add the butter to the same pan and melt over a medium heat. Add the spinach and fry until it's softened and all the water has been cooked off. Season with black pepper. Add the wine and cook until reduced by half. Add the cream and mustard, mixing well. Add the lemon zest. Bring the sauce to the boil and cook for 5 minutes until thickened.

Return the salmon fillets to the pan and cook for 1 minute in the sauce.

To serve, spoon some of the sauce onto the plates, top with a salmon fillet, then garnish with chives. Serve at once.

This is a really indulgent dish, which I enjoy serving at dinner parties. It always makes my guests very happy indeed!

BAKED FISH WITH A SECRET INGREDIENT

SERVES 6

6 x 200g (7 oz) skinless salmon/white fish fillets, or a combination of the two
Salt
4 lemon slices

SAUCE
125ml (½ cup) oil
1 small onion, roughly chopped
1–2 celery stalks, roughly chopped
½ yellow pepper, cut into strips
1 small carrot sliced
1 medium-hot, long red or green chilli
7 garlic cloves, halved
1 tomato, roughly chopped
150–200ml (5–7 fl oz) ketchup
1 tsp sugar
½ tsp pareve chicken stock powder (optional)
125ml (½ cup) water
1 heaped tbsp chopped coriander

*Pareve is the term for food that doesn't contain milk or meat, since in Kosher cooking we don't mix meat and milk or meat and fish.

Salt the fish: Rinse the fish fillets and pat dry. Place in a bowl, season with salt and chill in the fridge for 4 hours or overnight.

Preheat the oven to 180°C/350°F.

Make the sauce: Heat the oil in a small saucepan over a medium heat. Add onion, celery, pepper and carrot. Cut a slit lengthways in the chilli and add. Cook, stirring now and then, until the vegetables have slightly softened. Add garlic and cook for another minute.

Add tomato, ketchup, sugar, chicken stock powder and water. Stir well, bring to the boil and cook for 2 minutes. Add the chopped coriander, stir and remove from heat. Taste and season accordingly; you want it to be sweet and sour.

Bake the fish: Arrange the fish fillets (skinned side down) in a deep baking tray. Pour over the sauce evenly, then top with the lemon slices. Bake for 30 minutes, until the fish and vegetables begin to brown. Serve at once with fresh bread or Challah (see p.183).

I usually serve this special dish for Shabbat or for festivals. Everyone, whether a grown-up or a child, loves the flavour of the dish, with its special 'secret ingredient' — ketchup! Once we had guests coming for Shabbat who told me they never ate fish. I asked them just to try a little bit and they liked the dish so much that they ate three servings.

CRISPY HOME-MADE FISH FINGERS

SERVES 4

750g (1lb 10oz) skinless fillets of haddock or cod (cut from the middle part of the fish)
1 tbsp salt

Oil for frying
40g (4 tbsp) butter

COATING
140g (1 cup) flour seasoned with black pepper
4 eggs, beaten with 3 tbsp milk or water
200g (7oz) panko breadcrumbs or dry breadcrumbs

TARTARE SAUCE
100g (3½ oz) shallots, finely chopped
100g (3½ oz) gherkins, finely chopped
100g (3½ oz) small capers, well rinsed
A handful of chopped parsley
2 heaped tbsp mayonnaise
2 tbsp sour cream
¼ tsp mustard
Grated zest of ½ lemon

Salt the fish: Place the fillets on a dish and sprinkle with the salt. Cover with film and chill in the fridge for at least 2 hours.

Make the tartare sauce: Mix all the ingredients together.

Prepare the fish: Cut the fish fillets lengthways into strips, then across into 'fingers' around 10 x 2cm (4 x ¾in).

Coat the fish fingers in the seasoned flour. Holding one fish finger in your right hand, dip it in the beaten egg. Holding the fish finger in your left hand, coat it in the panko breadcrumbs. Repeat the process until all the fish fingers have been coated.

Fry the fish: Pour the oil into a frying pan to a depth of 5mm (¼in) and heat it. Once the oil is bubbling, add the fish fingers and then the butter. Fry the fish in batches for around 5 minutes, turning over halfway through, until golden on both sides. Drain on kitchen paper.

Serve with tartare sauce and the Cucumber Radish Salad (see p.93).

"There is nothing more English than fish and chips (fries). Rather than using a traditional batter, I prefer this crispy panko coating. Making your own tartare sauce is very easy — and it goes wonderfully with the fish fingers."

NOSTALGIC KINDERGARTEN FISHBALLS

SERVES 5–6

FOR THE FISH BALLS

- 2 large onions, chopped
- 4 tbsp oil
- 1kg (2lb 4oz) skinless fillet of cod or any other firm-fleshed white fish, and minced (chopped)
- 3 slices white bread, crusts trimmed, dampened with water, squeezed dry and grated
- 2 eggs
- 1 garlic clove, crushed
- 1 tbsp lemon juice
- 1 heaped tsp salt
- Ground pepper
- 2 heaped tsp sugar
- 3–4 tbsp matzo meal

FOR THE SAUCE

- 4 tbsp oil
- 3 tbsp tomato paste
- 2 tbsp ketchup
- 2 garlic cloves, crushed
- 1 tsp salt
- 1–2 tbsp sugar
- ½ tsp paprika
- ½ tsp ground turmeric
- Ground pepper
- 2 tsp pareve* chicken stock powder
- 1 litre (1 quart) boiling water, plus a little more if needed

*Pareve is the term for food that doesn't contain milk or meat, since in Kosher cooking we don't mix meat and milk or meat and fish.

Make the fish balls: Fry the chopped onion in the oil over low to medium heat, stirring often, until light golden. Sieve the fried onion and squeeze out excess oil. Using a hand blender, coarsely mince the onion.

Place the fried onion and all the remaining fish ball ingredients in a bowl, adding ground pepper to taste. Mix well, using your hands.

With wet hands, shape the mixture into fish balls, around the size of ping pong balls.

Make the sauce: Place all the sauce ingredients in a large saucepan, adding ground pepper to taste. Bring to the boil. Add in the fish balls, return to the boil, reduce the heat, cover and simmer for 20 minutes. Serve with white rice.

Fried fishcakes variation:
Alternatively, shape the fish mixture with oiled hands into fishcakes, around 6–7cm across and fry these in hot oil until browned on both sides and serve these plain, without the sauce. A nice touch, which I remember fondly, is to coat the fishcakes in breadcrumbs before frying.

When I was a little girl at kindergarten, these fish balls were my favourite lunch. As I was playing, I could smell them cooking and would wait impatiently for them to be ready. They were served either poached in this sauce or as fried fishcakes — I loved them either way! It's taken me years of recipe testing to recreate them, but this recipe takes me back to those happy days.

'MJUJIM' – MARRIED SARDINES

MAKES 4

8 fresh sardines, cleaned and butterflied
Salt
Flour, for coating
Black pepper
Oil for frying
Butter, for frying (optional)
Lemon wedges, to serve

FILLING

1 fresh sardine, filleted and skinned
A handful of chopped coriander leaves
3–4 garlic cloves, crushed
6 tbsp oil
1 level tbsp sweet paprika
½ tbsp hot paprika

Salt the sardines: Sprinkle a little salt over each butterflied sardine on both sides. Chill them in the fridge for an hour.

Make the filling: Chop the filleted sardine very finely. Mix it with the remaining filling ingredients.

Assemble and fry the sardines: Place 4 of the butterflied sardines skin side down on a plate or chopping board. Spread the filling evenly over the flesh side of each sardine. Top each one with a butterflied sardine, skin facing up.

Season the flour with black pepper. Take each sardine 'sandwich' and coat on both sides in the flour.

Heat a little oil — just enough to form a thin layer — in a frying pan over medium-high heat. Fry the sardines on both sides until golden-brown. As you fry the sardines, add a little butter to the oil for extra flavour and crispness. Serve at once with lemon wedges on the side.

This is a truly wonderful way to eat sardines. 'Mjujim' means 'married' in Moroccan, so the name is a playful reference to the pairs of butterflied sardines which are joined together. The combination of the crispy fried fish and the spicy filling with a squeeze of lemon juice is just the best!

HAMSI

SERVES 4–5

30–36 fresh anchovies, gutted
Salt
Cornflour (corn starch) or flour, for coating
40g (4 tbsp) butter
Lemon wedges, to serve

Sprinkle the anchovies lightly with salt. Set aside in the fridge for 1 hour. Pat dry lightly and coat in corn starch or flour on both sides.

Heat the butter in a 24cm (9½ in) frying pan. Carefully arrange the anchovies in a single layer in the pan with the heads facing outwards and the tails overlapping in the centre. The arrangement should resemble the spokes of a wheel.

Fry the anchovies for 5 minutes on one side. Place a large, flat plate on top of the frying pan. Quickly invert the pan and return the anchovies to it at once. Fry for a few minutes more, till golden-brown on the other side. Serve at once with lemon wedges.

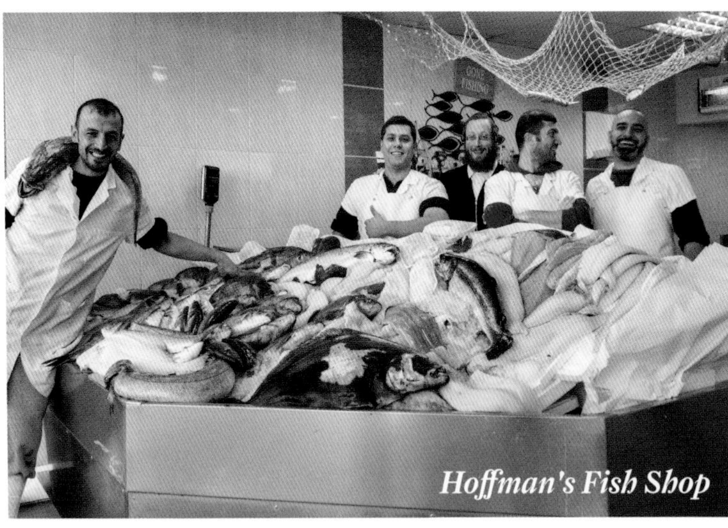

Hoffman's Fish Shop

I was first told about hamsi by a Turkish fishmonger at my kosher fish shop in London. It sounded so interesting that I tried making it at home myself. I love the shape the anchovies make — it's such a striking dish and tastes great too.

الاعمال العامة

Quick
& Easy

ANAMARK WALNUT
GROWER • PROCESSOR
PREMIUM CALIFORNIA SHELLED WALNUTS PRODUCT OF U.S.A.
תערובת לביבות
סחלב
קפה ירוק טהור טבעי
Natural pure green coffee
14.00 ₪

FOODWISE

Thinking back to what was on offer in the local food shops in Tel Aviv during the '70s, it was limited compared to today's abundance, but we enjoyed what we had.

Our milk came in plastic bags which we placed in special jugs. You snipped off its tip with scissors to open the bag. This took skill. If the hole was too small the milk shot out, too big and it splashed out! We called the sliced cheese we used in sandwiches 'yellow cheese'. There was a chocolate drink made from sterilised milk sold in glass bottles with a picture of a man wearing a funny hat on the label. It tasted heavenly. On the street next to our house was a shop that sold cold cuts — turkey, pastrami, salami. It didn't come in vacuum packs but was freshly sliced to order. I enjoyed watching the shopkeeper slice these huge pieces of meat on a gleaming metal slicer. I was hypnotised by the sound and sight of it. As the eldest child, my mum used to send me out to buy cold cuts. This was a mistake. On the way home I couldn't resist sneaking a slice or two into my mouth....

We often used chicken's feet when we made chicken soup. Not only did the feet make the soup taste great but we loved to suck the flesh off the bones.

We lived in an era when so many things were new and exciting. I remember the first dairy treats which arrived in the stores — Prili, a sweet yoghurt with real fruit in it. It wasn't cheap so my clever mum used to mix yoghurt or sour cream with raspberry syrup which, to tell the truth, tasted even better than the original. Every day I bought myself a Krembo. I was addicted to these round cookies with creamy vanilla or coffee-flavoured egg white topping coated with chocolate.

Even the medicines tasted wonderful! My favourite was an antibiotic called Penibrin. Any little pain was an excuse to go to see a doctor and beg, 'Please, can I have Penibrin?' It was sweet, delicious and I was hooked. My mum told me that when I was two years old, I snuck to the fridge and drank a whole bottle. My poor parents rushed me to the hospital.

We shopped at small grocery shops which sold a limited range of basic goods. I still remember the first time I visited a supermarket. It was the Kol-Bo Shalom's supermarket, housed in the tallest building in Tel Aviv. The supermarket was vast. It was the first time I had ever seen a shopping trolley! To my excitement, my father put me in the trolley and we strolled around. The shelves were packed with foods which I had never seen before: dulce de leche, canned spinach (which reminded me of Popeye), breakfast cereals that I'd never even heard of in brightly coloured boxes. My father, who loved to try new foods, was as excited as me. We marvelled at the variety and abundance of goods and brought lots of treats back home to the family.

EJJA

SERVES 5–6

- 4 large eggs
- 1 large onion, coarsely grated and squeezed dry
- 1 courgette (zucchini), finely grated and squeezed dry
- 1 small potato, peeled, finely grated and squeezed dry (optional)
- 2 tbsp chopped dill
- 2 tbsp chopped parsley
- 2 tbsp chopped coriander
- Salt and pepper
- 3 tbsp oil
- 30g (2 tbsp) butter

Beat the eggs with the onion, courgette (zucchini), potato, dill, parsley and coriander until well mixed. Season with salt and pepper.

Heat the oil and butter in a 24cm (9½ in) frying pan over medium heat. Pour in the egg mixture.

Fry for 30 seconds, then reduce the heat and fry gently, uncovered, for 20 minutes until set on top. Invert the ejja using a large plate and return it to the pan, cooking it over medium heat for 30 seconds. Then reduce the heat and fry over a low heat for 5 minutes more.

Serve warm or at room temperature with Tzatziki (see p.74).

Filled with herbs and good things, this is an Iraqi omelette. For Shav'uot, when we eat dairy ingredients, I like to add feta to it. Served with salad, it makes a truly tasty meal.

LG
ELECTRA

POTATO LATKES

MAKES 10 LATKES

1kg (2lb 4oz) floury potatoes (I use Maris Pipers)
1 onion
2 eggs
2 tbsp flour (I like to use potato flour)
½ tsp salt
Black pepper
1 tsp sugar

FOR FRYING
Oil
20g (1½ tbsp) butter (optional)

APPLE SAUCE DIP
5–6 Granny Smith apples, peeled and chopped
100g (½ cup) sugar
juice of ½ lemon
1 tsp vanilla essence
½ tsp ground cinnamon
125ml (½ cup) water
Pinch of salt

SOUR CREAM DIP
200g (7oz) sour cream
6 tbsp chopped spring onion (scallion), green part only
½ tsp onion soup mix
Pinch of salt

TIP: For fluffier latkes add ⅓ tsp baking powder to the mixture with the flour.

Make the Apple Sauce Dip: Place all the ingredients together in a small saucepan, bring to the boil over a medium heat, reduce the heat and cook covered for 15–20 minutes, stirring now and then, until the apple has softened. Blend using a hand blender to your preferred consistency. Set aside.

Make the Sour Cream Dip: Mix the Sour Cream Dip ingredients together, cover and store in the fridge until serving.

Make the Latkes: Peel and coarsely grate the potatoes. Squeeze dry. Coarsely grate the onion and squeeze dry.

Place the grated potato and onion, eggs, flour, salt, pepper and sugar in a bowl. Using your hands, mix together thoroughly.

Pour oil in a large frying pan to a depth of just over 1cm (⅓in). Heat over medium high and add the butter (if using) when the oil is hot.

Make each latke by taking a heaped tablespoon of the potato mixture and rounding it using a second spoon. Add the latke at once to the hot oil and gently press down with a back of a spoon to flatten slightly. Repeat the process, spacing them well apart, until the pan is full, frying them in batches. As the latkes fry, turn them and cook until they become golden brown on both sides. Remove and drain on kitchen paper.

Serve the warm latkes at once with the dips.

Hanukkah celebrates the rededication of the Holy Temple. Miraculously, during this event, the sacred oil, which was only enough to light the lamps in the temple for one day, lasted for eight days. So, for the festival of Hanukkah, we light lamps or candles and celebrate by eating foods fried in oil, like doughnuts or potato latkes. Each Jewish community in different countries around the world has its own versions of latkes; this recipe is for Ashkenazi latkes. Served warm, these simple potato fritters are absolutely irresistible!

LIMI'S SCHNITZEL & PETYA'S TWIST

SERVES 6

6–8 chicken breast fillets (around 1kg)
Oil for frying

FLOUR COATING
150g (5oz) flour
¼ tsp garlic powder
½ tsp turmeric
Salt and black pepper

EGG COATING
4 large eggs
3 tbsp water
3 tbsp soy sauce
1–2 tsp mustard

BREADCRUMB COATING
300g (10oz) dried breadcrumbs
A handful of finely chopped parsley leaves (optional)

Petya

Prepare the chicken schnitzel: If using whole chicken breast fillets, slice the thick part of the fillet, opening it out, then cut into two. Place the pieces between two sheets of cling film/plastic wrap. Pound gently and evenly with a meat hammer until just under 1cm (around ⅓in) thick. Repeat with the remaining pieces.

Mix the ingredients for the flour coating. Thoroughly coat the chicken pieces in the flour, lightly shaking off excess, and set aside.

In a separate bowl, whisk together the egg coating ingredients. In a separate bowl, mix the breadcrumbs and parsley.

Dip the chicken pieces in the beaten egg mixture, letting any excess drip off. Coat thoroughly in breadcrumbs, shaking off any excess.

Cook the schnitzel: Pour oil to a depth of 2cm (around ¾ in) into a deep frying pan and heat over medium-high heat. Fry the chicken in batches for around 90 seconds till golden, then turn and fry until golden on the other side. Repeat the process for another 40 seconds on each side, until golden-brown and cooked through. Drain on kitchen paper. Repeat until all the schnitzels have been fried.

Petyas's Twist: Use 6 large eggs for the egg coating instead of just 4. Prepare as above but dip the breadcrumb-coated schnitzel once more into the beaten egg mixture just before frying. This twist gives you extra-soft, tender schnitzel. Try it!

TIP: There is a simple trick to avoid sticky hands. Use your right hand to egg coat and your left hand for breadcrumbs. I've taught a lot of my neighbours this useful tip and they are very grateful!

I've always made classic crispy schnitzel and didn't think there was any other way of cooking them. One day, however, Petya, my lovely kitchen assistant, told me that she dipped the schnitzel in the egg once more before frying them and that this makes them deliciously tender. Intrigued, I tried Petya's twist and she was right — schnitzels cooked her way stay soft, even the next day. My kids enjoyed them so much that they always ask for 'Petya's schnitzel'!

THE WRAP ON THE PLANE

MAKES 6

250ml (1 cup) sweet chilli sauce
1 heaped tsp curry powder
6 fried chicken schnitzels (see recipe on previous page)
6 tortillas

Mix the chilli sauce and curry powder thoroughly. Generously spread this spiced sauce on both sides of each schnitzel, coating thoroughly. Slice into pieces around 1.5cm (½ in) thick.

Briefly heat the tortillas in the microwave. Wrap the schnitzel pieces in the tortillas, forming 6 wraps, and eat at once.

My sons (from left) Srulik, Yoeli and David

Once on a long, tiring flight back from L.A. we were pleasantly surprised to get a tasty curried-chicken tortilla wrap, instead of the normal bland airplane food. My boys love spicy food, and back in London they asked me to make it again for them. So I came up with my version of the 'Wrap on the Plane'. Now, when we have schnitzel they often ask for this. It's an excellent way of using up leftover schnitzel.

LEMON PAPRIKA CAULIFLOWER

SERVES 4

- 700g (1lb 9oz) cauliflower florets, frozen or fresh
- 3–4 tbsp oil
- 2 garlic cloves, sliced
- 1 tsp sweet paprika
- 1 tsp chicken or vegetable stock powder
- Salt and pepper
- 4 tbsp hot chicken or vegetable stock
- Juice of 1 lemon

If using frozen cauliflower, add the florets to a saucepan of boiling water. As soon as the water returns to the boil, remove and drain.

Heat the oil in a saucepan over medium heat. Add the garlic and fry for a minute, then add the cauliflower, stirring to coat well with the oil.

Mix the paprika, stock powder, and salt and pepper with the stock. Add this to the cauliflower, cover the pan, reduce the heat and cook for 5 minutes (for frozen) or 10 minutes (for fresh), until the cauliflower has softened. Add the lemon juice and cook uncovered over medium heat for a few minutes until the sauce has reduced by around half. Serve at once.

MUM'S PERFECT STEAK

SERVES 2

A small piece of lamb fat
2 rib-eye or frying steaks, each around 200g (7oz), at room temperature
1–2 tbsp olive oil
Salt and pepper

Heat a large, heavy-based frying pan over low heat. Add the lamb fat and allow it to brown and melt, coating the pan. Remove the browned fat and fight over who gets to eat it!

Increase the heat to medium high. Rub the olive oil over the steaks and season them with salt and pepper. Place the steaks in the frying pan; they should sizzle on contact with the pan.

For medium cooked steaks, fry the steaks without moving for 2 minutes. Turn the steaks over and cook for 1 minute. Set aside for 3 minutes in pan, then serve at once.

In Tel Aviv in the 1970s, steaks were a real treat. My mum would fry them in lamb fat, rather than butter, for kosher reasons. This gives them a wonderful rich flavour: I remember how my brothers and I would fight over who got to eat that delicious little bit of crispy browned lamb fat that was left at the end! The secret to cooking steaks well is to get the frying pan really hot. You want the steaks to sear when they hit the pan, forming a tasty crust.

CUMIN SPAGHETTI

SERVES 5

Salt
450g (1lb) spaghetti

SAUCE
3 tbsp oil
3 garlic cloves, crushed
1 tsp salt
1 tbsp sugar
2 tsp ground cumin
Ground black pepper
3 tbsp tomato paste
75–125ml (3–4 fl oz) boiling water

Bring a large saucepan of salted water to the boil. Add the spaghetti and cook until al dente.

Meanwhile, place all sauce ingredients in a large saucepan. Mix together, taste and adjust seasoning as needed. Over medium heat, bring to the boil. Once the sauce comes to the boil, reduce the heat and simmer for 2 minutes, then set aside.

Drain the spaghetti and add the warm spaghetti immediately to the sauce. Mix well, coating the spaghetti in the sauce, and serve at once.

Is there a better side dish to serve with steaks than fries? I think this cumin spaghetti is AMAZING with steak — try it and see!

SWEET AND SOUR COURGETTES

SERVES 6

- 2 tbsp oil
- 1 small onion, chopped
- 5 courgettes (zucchini) or 15 baby ones, cut into slices 1cm (around ½ in) thick
- 1 tomato, chopped
- A handful of chopped dill

SAUCE

- 2 tbsp tomato paste
- Salt and pepper
- 1 heaped tbsp sugar
- 1 tsp paprika
- 125ml (½ cup) chicken or vegetable stock

Mix the sauce ingredients. Taste and adjust to taste.

Heat the oil in a saucepan. Add the onion and fry, stirring, over medium low heat until softened and translucent.

Reduce the heat to low. Add the courgette (zucchini), tomato and dill. Pour in the sauce, cover and cook gently for 30 minutes, stirring now and then, until the courgettes (zucchini) are softened but retain some texture.

I like to serve this dish with white rice.

> "This is my mother's recipe. She served it with fried fish and rice for lunch on Fridays when we came back from the sea. It's a dish which brings back happy childhood memories."

COURGETTE FRITTERS

MAKES 10

- 3 large, dark green courgettes (zucchini), coarsely grated and squeezed dry
- 1 large onion, coarsely grated and squeezed dry
- 2 eggs
- 1 small potato, grated
- 2 tbsp chopped dill
- 2 tbsp chopped parsley
- 3–4 tbsp fine matzo meal
- Salt and pepper
- ¼ tsp ground cumin (optional)

FOR FRYING

- 5–6 tbsp oil
- 20g (1½ tbsp) butter

In a mixing bowl, thoroughly mix all the fritter ingredients together. If the mixture is too soft, add more matzo meal and mix in.

Add the oil to a large frying pan and heat over a medium heat, then add the butter. Using your hands or two spoons, shape portions of the fritter mixture into rounded, flat patties.

Fry the fritters in batches, adding a few at a time, taking care not to overcrowd the pan. Fry for around 2 minutes on each side, until golden. Drain on paper towels. When they are all cooked, serve at once.

These quick and easy fritters are best enjoyed while they are still warm from frying. They are a great way to eat vegetables — with the results enjoyed by meat-eaters and vegetarians alike.

SYRIAN RICE WITH NOODLES

SERVES 6

200g (around 1 cup) basmati rice
Oil for frying
100g (3½ oz) broken vermicelli noodles
1 garlic clove, unpeeled
Salt
500ml (2 cups) boiling water

Place the rice in a bowl, cover with cold water and gently stir with your hands a few times, then drain. Repeat the process twice more. This is to wash off excess starch.

Heat a saucepan for a minute over medium heat. Pour in enough oil to coat the bottom of the pan and heat through briefly.

Add the noodles, reduce the heat to low and gently stir the noodles, coating them in the oil. Fry for 9–10 minutes over a low heat, stirring now and then (they burn easily), until they darken to a rich brown colour.

Add the rice and mix in, coating it well with the oil. Add the garlic and season with salt.

Pour in the boiling water and stir gently to mix briefly but thoroughly. Bring to the boil and reduce the heat to low. Place a lid on the pan, cover with a clean kitchen towel, and cook for 15 minutes.

Turn off the heat. Leave the rice to stand covered for a further 15 minutes before serving.

This is a traditional Syrian dish, especially associated with Aleppo. Adding the noodles to the rice gives an extra dimension, making it more than just a side dish.

SWEET RICE CAKES

SERVES 8–10

200g (around 1 cup) basmati rice
375ml (1½ cups) boiling water
250ml (1 cup) freshly squeezed orange juice
6 eggs
200g (1 cup) sugar
¼ tsp ground cinnamon
½ tsp vanilla essence
Pinch of salt
125ml (½ cup) oil
125ml (½ cup) canned coconut milk

TOPPING

A sprinkle of Demerara (soft brown) sugar

Preheat the oven to 180°C/350°F. Grease a cake tin around 11 x 26cm (around 4 x 13in) or 10 mini loaf cases around 5.5 x 10cm (around 2 x 4in).

Put the rice and boiling hot water in a saucepan. Cover, bring to the boil, stir, then reduce the heat and cook covered for 10 minutes, until the water has been absorbed and the rice is cooked through. Transfer the rice to a large bowl to cool slightly.

Add the remaining ingredients to the rice and mix well using a fork. Pour the mixture into the cake tin or divide among the 10 mini loaf cases. Lightly sprinkle the surface of the cake with Demerara (soft brown) sugar.

Bake the large cake for 1 hour, until set and browned on top. If using the loaf cases, bake for 30 minutes. Cool on a rack. Serve warm or at room temperature.

Fifteen years ago, during Tisha B'av, towards the end of the fasting day, a neighbour kindly brought round a freshly baked sweet rice pie. I had never tasted one before. The smell was so tempting that I struggled to reach the end of the fast! When I finally tasted it, I was surprised that something that looked so simple could taste so good. Whenever I fast I always think of this pie. My family enjoys it so much that I make it throughout the year.

NEW YEAR LEEK FRITTERS (KARTI)

MAKES 10–12

2 tbsp oil, plus oil for frying
1 large onion, roughly chopped
8 leeks, white part only, roughly chopped
1 potato, peeled, boiled and mashed
1 egg
4–5 tbsp fine matzo meal
Salt and pepper
Oil for frying

Heat 2 tbsp oil in a saucepan over a medium-low heat. Fry the onion for 5 minutes, until translucent. Add the leek and mix. Reduce the heat to low, cover and cook, stirring now and then, for 10–15 minutes till softened; let the mixture cool.

Transfer to a sieve over a bowl and squeeze dry. Place the leek mixture on a chopping board and chop with a knife.

Place the mixture in a bowl, add the mashed potato, egg and matzo meal and mix well with your hands. Season with salt and pepper. The mixture should be firm; add more matzo meal if needed.

To form the fritters, take a portion of the mixture, shape into a ball and pat into a disc roughly 6cm (2½ in) in diameter and 1cm (⅓in) thick. Repeat the process until all the mixture has been used up.

Pour oil into a frying pan to a depth of just under 1cm (⅓in). Cook the fritters in batches until golden brown on both sides; drain on paper towels. Serve hot or at room temperature.

If making ahead, after frying, these latkes can be cooled and frozen in freezer-proof container and will keep well for a month.

Right: Leek and Chard fritters

NEW YEAR CHARD FRITTERS (SILKA)

MAKES 10

10 chard leaves
5–6 tbsp oil
1 large onion, chopped
1 small potato, peeled, boiled, mashed and cooled
1 egg
2–3 tbsp fine matzo meal
Salt and pepper

Cut the stalks off the chard leaves. Chop the stalks and shred the green leaves, keeping them separated.

Heat 3 tbsp of the oil in a frying pan over medium heat. Fry the onion for 5 minutes, until translucent. Add the chopped stalks and fry, stirring, till softened. Add the shredded leaves and fry, stirring constantly, till softened. Drain in a sieve.

Squeeze the chard mixture dry and chop it. Place in a bowl. Add the remaining ingredients, apart from the oil. Mix by hand to form a firm mixture, adding more matzo meal if needed.

Take small handfuls and shape into fritters around 6cm (2½ in) long.

Heat the remaining oil in a frying pan over medium high heat. Fry the fritters in batches until golden on both sides. Remove and drain on kitchen paper. Serve hot or at room temperature.

To freeze, store in an airtight container and use within 1 month.

Variation: Add 200g (7oz) minced (chopped) beef, frying it with the onion.

Both the leek and chard fritters are among the symbolic foods eaten at Rosh Hashanah (Jewish New Year) as a way of ensuring auspicious events in the year ahead. I always make plenty of both, because they disappear very quickly!

מחזור

My Kids Are Crazy For This

RAISING CHILDREN

When people ask me what I do, I reply that I'm a housewife and a mother. They respond: 'So, don't you work?'.

Looking after my children is a 24-hour job. We live in a world where value is measured in monetary terms so we tend to think of 'work' as something we earn money for. If I said that I looked after other people's children for 12 hours a day, it would be considered a job, but to look after my own is not.

Our culture is materialistic, where financial gain is regarded as the peak of achievement. We undervalue intangible, spiritual achievements. For me, to raise children well is priceless.

Boli Star
30
First Colouring Book
פיות
-20-
24 Colors
ג'מבו
12 Colors
25
DOUBLE SIX COLOR DOT DOMINOES
DOMINO
18
אותיות
15
P.H.244
Avocados

YOELI'S STUFFED PEPPERS (PILEP)

SERVES 6

6 large red or yellow peppers or 10 small light green peppers

FOR THE FILLING

100g (½ cup) basmati rice
3–4 tbsp oil
2–3 large onions, chopped
700g (1lb 8oz) minced lamb or beef
1 tsp chicken stock powder
1 tbsp tomato purée
Pinch of baharat spice mixture, optional)
1 tbsp chopped parsley (optional)
Salt and pepper

FOR THE SAUCE

3 tbsp oil
1 large onion, finely chopped
1 ltr (4 cups) warm water
200g (7oz) tomato paste
1–2 tbsp ketchup
1–2 tbsp sugar
½ tbsp sweet paprika
1 tbsp chicken stock powder
Salt and pepper

Prepare the rice for the filling: Soak the rice for 1 hour in cold water and drain.

Prepare the peppers: Cut the caps off, reserving half of them for use in the dish. De-seed the peppers thoroughly and set aside.

Make the filling: Heat the oil in a frying pan. Fry the onion gently, stirring often, until golden-brown. Take the reserved pepper lids and finely chop them, discarding the stalks. Mix with the fried onion, spoon off excess oil and set aside to cool. Once cool, mix together the meat, rice, onion mixture, chicken stock powder, tomato purée, baharat and parsley (if using). Season with salt and pepper and mix together thoroughly.

Stuff the peppers loosely with the filling; do not press it down. Reserve any leftover mince.

Make the sauce: Choose a lidded sauté pan which is deep enough for the peppers and will hold them snugly. Heat the oil in the pan. Add the onion and fry over a medium-low heat, stirring now and then, until it lightly browns. Remove the pan from direct heat. Place the filled peppers on top of the fried onion, either upright or on their side. Shape any leftover meat into meatballs and place between the peppers.

Mix the remaining sauce ingredients thoroughly and pour over the peppers. Bring to the boil, cover, reduce the heat to low and cook for 45 minutes, gently tilting the pan now and then. If they are standing, you will need to baste them with the sauce; if on their side, they will need turning over halfway through cooking.

Uncover and cook for a further 10 minutes to reduce the sauce. If you want to give a smoky flavour (and your pan is ovenproof) you can grill the dish in the oven at 200°C/400°F for 10 minutes to char the edges of the peppers. Serve.

A pot of stuffed peppers cooking on the hob is a wonderful mixture of colours, flavours and aromas that fill the house. This family recipe is the most delicious one. It's juicy and soft and from his first bite it became my son Yoeli's favourite dish. At the age of three, coming home from kindergarten, when he reached the door and smelt it cooking, he would shout out excitedly 'pilep, pilep'. In Hebrew the name for peppers is 'pilpel' — of course I never corrected him and that is how he calls them to this day.

ROCKET RACER

PITTA PIZZA

MAKES 4 PIZZAS

2 PITTAS

TOMATO TOPPING MIXTURE

3 tbsp tomato paste
2 tbsp ketchup
½ tsp garlic powder
1 tsp dried oregano
1 tsp sugar
Salt and pepper
2 tbsp olive oil

TOPPINGS

250g (9oz) grated cheese (mozzarella, Cheddar or a mixture)
Anchovy fillets
Olives
Basil leaves
Red pepper slices

Preheat the oven to 180°C/350°F.

Using a sharp knife, cut around the edge of one pitta and carefully pull it apart to form two circles. Repeat with the other pitta.

Mix together the ingredients for the tomato topping. Spread each pitta pizza evenly with the tomato mixture and top with your choice of topping ingredients.

Bake the pitta pizzas for 10 minutes until the cheese is bubbling and lightly golden.

In Israel every child knows Pitta Pizza. Quick and easy to make, this ingenious dish is a useful standby for tired, busy mums. A few years ago I decided to make proper pizza for my family. I went to a lot of trouble: making the dough, a rich tomato sauce, even going to Golders Green to buy a good kosher mozzarella. I was thrilled with what I'd made and waited for the compliments. 'Mum, we prefer your pitta pizza!' was what I got instead!

LIMI'S CHICKEN CURRY

SERVES 6

- 4 garlic cloves, peeled
- A piece of fresh ginger around 5–8cm (2–3in) in size, peeled and chopped
- 2 medium hot green chillies
- 4 tbsp oil, preferably coconut oil
- 1 onion, finely chopped
- ½ tsp ground turmeric
- 1 tbsp mild curry powder
- 1 tbsp garam masala
- 400g (14oz) can of chopped tomatoes
- 1–2 tbsp tomato paste
- 800ml (2¾ cup) canned coconut milk
- 100ml (3½ fl oz) vegetable or chicken stock
- 1 tsp sugar
- Salt
- 1kg (2lb 2oz) skinless, boneless chicken thighs, chopped into small pieces
- Handful of chopped coriander

Using a pestle and mortar, crush the garlic, ginger and chillies into a paste.

In a wide saucepan, heat the oil over medium heat. Fry the onion until golden, stirring now and then. Mix in the garlic paste, then the turmeric, curry powder and garam masala. Fry, stirring, for 30 seconds, to bring out their fragrance. Add the chopped tomatoes and tomato paste. Fry, stirring, for 2 minutes. Add the coconut milk and stock and stir to mix in. Season with sugar and salt, taste and adjust as desired.

Bring the curry sauce to the boil. Add the chicken and return to the boil. Reduce the heat to low. Cover and cook for 30 minutes, until the chicken is cooked through. Add the coriander and cook uncovered for 10 minutes to reduce the sauce.

Serve with basmati rice, Onion Bhaji (see following page) and Mint Sauce (see following page).

My boys love spicy food, especially Indian. Unusually for Orthodox Hassidic Jewish kids, they know all about onion bhaji, chicken tikka masala and samosas. They first discovered Indian food when we took them for family meals at Mattancherry, a kosher Indian restaurant in Golders Green. When (sadly) Mattancherry closed down, my kids begged me to cook them Indian food at home. Luckily, my gardener Peter from India, kindly taught me some recipes which I've adopted into my repertoire. This chicken curry and onion bhajis are a real treat!

ONION BHAJI

SERVES 6

3 large onions
1 potato
2 green chillies, deseeded and very finely chopped
1 heaped tbsp coriander seeds
1 tsp cumin seeds
Salt
210g (7½ oz) gram (chickpea) flour
3 tbsp cold water
Oil for frying

TIP: As you are handling raw chillies in this recipe, either wear gloves or be very careful to wash your hands thoroughly afterwards.

Peel the onions and halve lengthways. Trim off the root end from each onion half, then slice across into 7mm (around ¼ in) slices. Peel the potato, halve lengthways and slice very finely across.

Place the onions, potato, chillies, coriander, cumin seeds and salt in a large bowl. Use your hands to mix together well, firmly crushing the mixture to squeeze out the juices. Gradually add the gram flour and cold water, mixing together with your hands, so that it absorbs the moisture from the vegetables and forms a thick, sticky batter. Add 1–2 tbsp water if the mixture seems too dry.

Pour oil to a depth of 2cm (¾in) in a deep frying pan and heat over medium-high. When the oil is hot, take a tbsp of the onion mixture and press with another spoon to form a fritter shape. Add to the oil. Repeat the process, frying the onion bhaji in batches until golden brown on all sides. Remove with a slotted spoon and drain on kitchen paper. Eat warm with Mint Sauce.

MINT SAUCE

MAKES AROUND 125ML (½ CUP)

1 tsp sugar
4 tbsp boiling water
4 tbsp white wine vinegar
2 handfuls of mint leaves
Pinch of salt
2 tbsp ketchup

Mix the sugar with the boiling water, allow to cool, then mix with the vinegar. Place the mint leaves on a chopping board. Sprinkle with a pinch of salt and finely chop. Mix the mint leaves with the sugar mixture, then add ketchup and mix together. Taste and adjust the seasoning as required.

EGG-FRIED RICE

SERVES 5–6

- 4 tbsp vegetable oil
- 2 tbsp sesame oil
- 5 spring onions (scallions), green part only, roughly chopped
- 3 garlic cloves, peeled but left whole
- 2 portions of cooked chilled Limi's Rice (see p.385)

EGG MIXTURE

- 2 tbsp oil
- 1 tbsp sesame oil
- 2 eggs, beaten
- 2 tbsp soy sauce

Fry the rice: Heat both oils in a wok over medium heat. Add the spring onion (scallions) and garlic and stir-fry for 1 minute until slightly softened. Add the cold rice, mixing in well, and stir-fry 5–10 minutes until the rice is fragrant and crispy.

Add the eggs: Make a hollow in the middle of the rice. Whisk the oil, sesame oil and beaten eggs together briefly, then mix into the fried rice. Turn off the heat, mix in the soy sauce, discard the garlic cloves and serve at once.

TIP: Bear in mind that the rice needs to be cooked in advance and chilled before frying, so prepare the rice ahead of time.

SRULIK'S SWEET AND SOUR CHICKEN

SERVES 5–6

1kg (2lb 4oz) skinless chicken breast fillets, chopped into 2cm (¾in) square pieces
Oil for deep frying

BATTER

4 eggs, whisked
1 tsp salt
100g (¾ cup) flour
2 heaped tbsp cornflour (cornstarch)
2 tbsp cold water

SWEET AND SOUR GLAZE

125ml (½ cup) smooth apricot jam
6 tbsp ketchup
3 tbsp soy sauce
4 tbsp Demerara (soft brown) sugar
2 tbsp sweet chilli sauce
1 tsp garlic powder
1 tsp grated root ginger (optional)
3–4 tbsp vinegar
125ml (½ cup) boiling water
1 onion, roughly chopped

GARNISH

5 spring onions (scallions), sliced
Sesame seeds

Make the batter: Whisk the ingredients until thoroughly mixed into a smooth batter.

Make the glaze: Mix the apricot jam, ketchup, soy sauce, sugar, chilli sauce, garlic powder, ginger (if using) and vinegar. Taste and sweeten to taste, if need be.

Cook the chicken: Heat the oil in a deep saucepan over medium-high heat. Check that the oil is hot enough by inserting the handle of a wooden spoon in it. If bubbles form around it, the oil is ready.

Coat the chicken cubes in the batter. Deep fry in batches for 1–2 minutes, turning, until pale golden on all sides. Remove with a slotted spoon and drain on kitchen paper.

Place the glaze mixture in a large saucepan with the boiling water. Bring to the boil, taste to check the seasoning, then turn off the heat. Add the chopped onion and mix lightly. Add the fried chicken to the sauce and return to the boil. Reduce the heat and simmer for 5 minutes, stirring now and then to coat the chicken pieces in the sauce.

Garnish with spring onions (scallions) and a sprinkling of sesame seeds. Serve with Egg-fried Rice (see previous page).

My youngest son, Srulik, is addicted to Sweet and Sour Chicken: he is always asking me to cook it. But it's a lot of work, so I don't make it that often. He's found a great way of motivating me, however. Whenever we go to a Chinese restaurant he tells me, 'Mummy, your sweet and sour chicken is better than the restaurant's', Flattery gets you everywhere!

MEATBALLS SPAGHETTI

SERVES 5–6

MEATBALLS

800g (1lb 12oz) minced (chopped) meat — I use a 50/50 mixture of beef and lamb or beef and chicken
Salt and pepper
1 egg
3 garlic cloves, chopped
40g (½ cup) breadcrumbs
1 tbsp olive oil
Handful of chopped parsley
1 tbsp ketchup (optional)

Flour, for coating
Olive oil for frying

SAUCE

4 tbsp olive oil
1 onion, chopped
2 garlic cloves, chopped
Pinch of dried chilli flakes
125ml dry red wine
2 tomatoes, grated
3 tbsp tomato paste
500–750ml (2–3 cups) chicken stock
1–2 tbsp sugar
Salt and pepper
Handful of chopped parsley

Freshly cooked spaghetti, to serve

Make the meatballs: Thoroughly mix together the meatball ingredients and form into small meatballs, slightly smaller than a ping pong ball. Roll the meatballs lightly in flour to coat.

Pour enough olive oil in a frying pan to coat its surface. Heat the oil over medium heat. Add the meatballs in batches and fry until just lightly brown on all sides. Remove, and drain on kitchen paper.

Make the sauce: Heat the olive oil over medium heat in a saucepan. Add the onion and fry till golden, around 10–15 minutes. Add garlic and fry briefly until fragrant. Mix in the chilli flakes, add the red wine and cook until most of the wine has been cooked down. Add all the remaining ingredients except the parsley. Mix, taste and adjust flavours.

Bring the sauce to the boil. Add the meatballs, mix and bring back to the boil. Reduce the heat, cover and cook for 30 minutes. Towards the end of the cooking time, add the parsley.

Serve the meatball sauce on top of the spaghetti.

TIP: Alternatively, make the meatballs without the egg and, without frying them first, poach them in the sauce.

I have fond memories of spaghetti with meatballs. The first time I encountered spaghetti with meatballs was in the children's film 'The Lady and the Tramp'. Children love this dish — there's something therapeutic about breaking open the meatballs and mixing them into the spaghetti. It's fun!

PANCAKES

MAKES 12 PANCAKES

DRY INGREDIENTS
190g (1½ cups) self-raising flour
1½ tsp baking powder
4 tbsp sugar
Pinch of salt

WET INGREDIENTS
150ml (5 fl oz) milk
100ml (3½ fl oz) leben (buttermilk)
1 tsp vanilla essence
2 eggs
60g (¼ cup) butter, melted

Oil or melted butter for frying

Maple syrup to serve

Place the dry ingredients in a mixing bowl and mix together briefly. In a separate bowl, whisk together the wet ingredients.

Pour the wet ingredients into the dry ones and whisk together lightly and briefly to form a thick batter. Take care not to over-mix, as you don't want to remove all the air.

To fry the pancakes, heat a pancake pan over low heat. Brush it lightly with oil or melted butter. Pour in a small ladleful of batter, tilting the pan or spreading the batter with a spatula to spread it out in a circle. Fry until little bubbles form on the surface. Check that it has browned underneath, then turn and fry briefly to brown on other side. Repeat the process with the remaining batter.

Serve pancakes warm, with maple syrup on the side.

"This is my children's ultimate breakfast!"

COOKIE-MEN – BEST CHOCOLATE CHIP COOKIES

MAKES 26 COOKIES

400g (3 cups) flour, sifted
1 tsp salt
1 tsp bicarbonate of soda

225g (1 cup) melted butter
150g (¾ cup) demerara sugar
150g (¾ cup) sugar
1 egg
2 tsp vanilla essence
1 tsp rum essence

50g (2 oz) good-quality dark chocolate, chopped
50g (2 oz) good-quality milk chocolate, chopped
50g (2 oz) good-quality white chocolate, chopped
50g (2 oz) dark or milk chocolate chips

Place the flour, salt and bicarbonate of soda in a bowl and mix until combined.

In a second large bowl, stir together the melted butter, both sugars, the egg and vanilla and rum essences, until combined.

Add the flour mixture to the butter mixture and mix together, using your hands or a spoon, to form a soft, sticky dough.

Mix together the chocolate pieces. Add two-thirds of these to the dough and gently but thoroughly mix in, using your hands. Cover with cling film and chill the cookie mixture in the fridge for an hour to firm up.

Preheat oven to 180°C/350°F. Line 2 baking trays with baking parchment.

Shape the cookie dough into ping-pong sized balls. Place these, spaced well apart, on the lined trays. Gently press a few chocolate pieces into the top of each cookie dough ball, taking care not to flatten the balls.

Bake for 10-12 minutes until the cookies are golden. Remove from the oven and allow to cool and set before transferring from the baking trays.

TIP: If you want your cookies to be extra crisp and stay fresh for longer, see Limi's Notes and Tips p.392.

The Cookie Men chain had outlets in shopping centres in Tel Aviv selling their huge, freshly baked cookies. You could always track down a branch in the mall by following the tempting scent of baking cookies! Their trademark biscuits were generously filled with chocolate — delightfully crisp at the edges, while soft in the middle. This is my version of these addictively good choc-chip cookies.

HOME-MADE ENERGY BARS

MAKES AROUND 15 BARS

DRY INGREDIENTS

60g (½ cup) wholemeal flour
50g (⅜ cup) plain white flour
90g (1 cup) rolled oats
80g (⅘ cup) desiccated coconut
120g (⅗ cup) soft light brown sugar
1 tsp bicarbonate of soda
½ tsp ground cinnamon
60g (2oz) golden raisins, each halved (optional)
150g (5oz) large chocolate chips

WET INGREDIENTS

100g (½ cup) butter
1 tbsp honey
6 tbsp maple syrup

Preheat oven to 160°C/325°F. Oil a shallow 20 x 30cm (8 x 12in) baking pan.

Mix all the dry ingredients apart from the chocolate chips in a mixing bowl.

In a saucepan over medium heat, gently warm together the wet ingredients, stirring all the time, until the butter has melted.

Pour the mixture while still warm into the dry mixture. Add the chocolate chips and mix in.

Transfer the mixture to the tin and press it down firmly. Bake for 30–40 minutes until light gold. Cool completely, then slice into bars. Store in an airtight container; they will keep for a week.

"It makes me happy that my sons take my own home-made snacks to school — they are much healthier and I guarantee that they are much tastier than shop-bought ones."

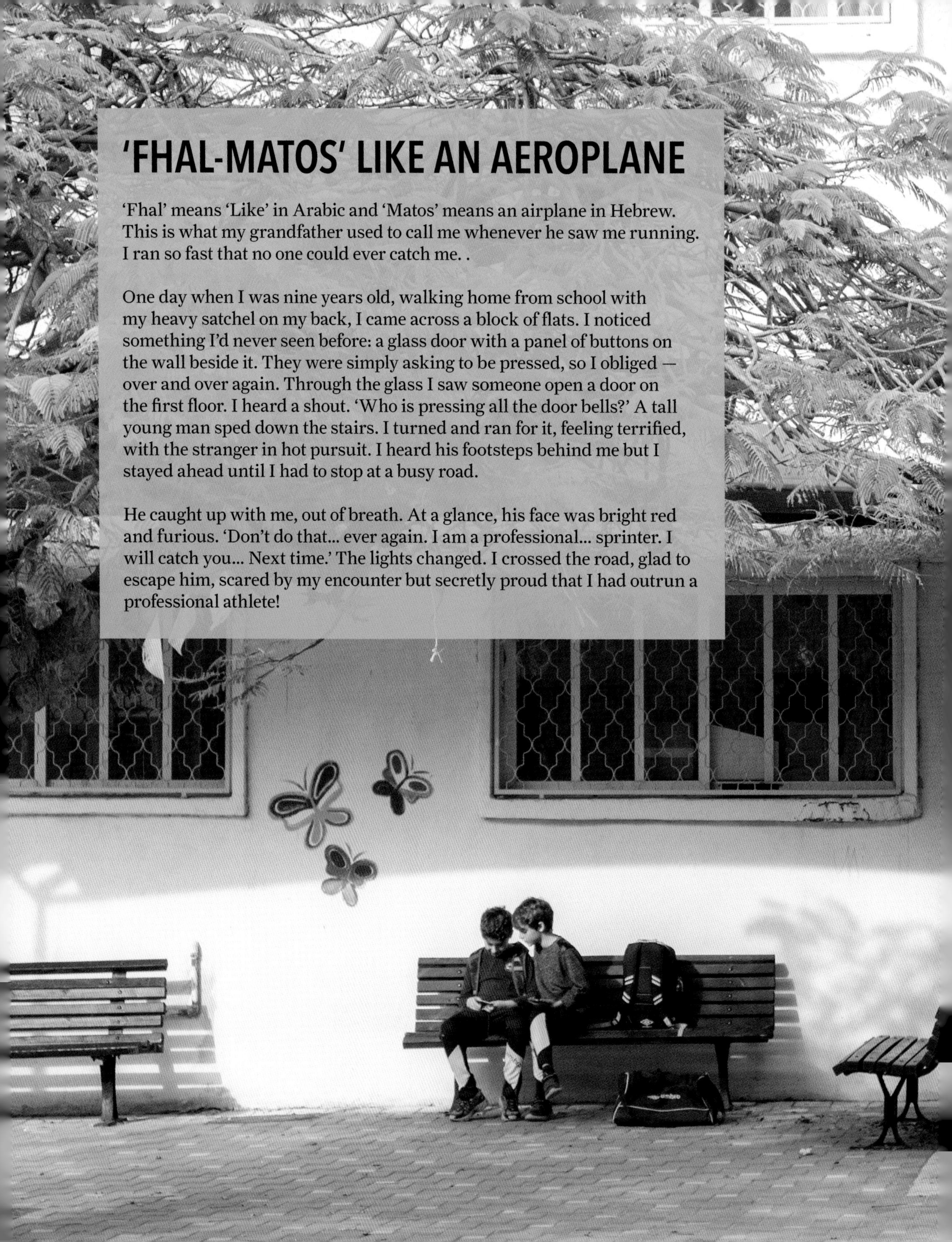

'FHAL-MATOS' LIKE AN AEROPLANE

'Fhal' means 'Like' in Arabic and 'Matos' means an airplane in Hebrew. This is what my grandfather used to call me whenever he saw me running. I ran so fast that no one could ever catch me. .

One day when I was nine years old, walking home from school with my heavy satchel on my back, I came across a block of flats. I noticed something I'd never seen before: a glass door with a panel of buttons on the wall beside it. They were simply asking to be pressed, so I obliged — over and over again. Through the glass I saw someone open a door on the first floor. I heard a shout. 'Who is pressing all the door bells?' A tall young man sped down the stairs. I turned and ran for it, feeling terrified, with the stranger in hot pursuit. I heard his footsteps behind me but I stayed ahead until I had to stop at a busy road.

He caught up with me, out of breath. At a glance, his face was bright red and furious. 'Don't do that... ever again. I am a professional... sprinter. I will catch you... Next time.' The lights changed. I crossed the road, glad to escape him, scared by my encounter but secretly proud that I had outrun a professional athlete!

עיריית תל - אביב - יפו
מינהל החינוך, התרבות והספורט ● משרד החינוך
בית הספר הממלכתי הקהילתי
ע"ש
"דוד ילין"

LIMI'S BEST EVER HOME-MADE RUGELACH

MAKES 64 RUGELACH (ENOUGH FOR 10 KIDS!)

DOUGH
35g fresh yeast or 3½ tsp dried
200g (1 cup) sugar
1kg (2lb 4oz) strong white bread flour
Around 325ml (1¼ cups) lukewarm water
200g (1 cup) soft margarine or softened butter
3 eggs
1 tsp vanilla essence
1 heaped tsp salt

FILLING
500g (1lb 2oz) good quality chocolate spread*
4 tbsp ground cinnamon

or Home-made Chocolate Rugelach Filling see p.391

EGG GLAZE
1 egg, beaten with 1 tbsp water

SUGAR SYRUP
400g (2 cups) sugar
375ml (1½ cups) water
1 tsp freshly squeezed lemon juice

*Warm chocolate spread in microwave for approx. 20sec before using

Make the dough: Crumble the yeast into the bowl of a stand mixer, or sprinkle in if using dried. Add 1 tsp sugar, 1 tbsp flour and 4 tbsp of lukewarm water and stir gently. Cover with a clean kitchen towel and leave for 15 minutes, until the yeast has become active and frothy.

Add the remaining flour, margarine, eggs and vanilla essence to the yeast. Using the dough hook on a medium speed, gradually add the remaining lukewarm water, using just 4 tbsp at first and incorporating between additions. Once the mixture is smooth, add the salt. Mix for 5 more minutes to make a soft, slightly sticky dough. Using your hands, oil both the bowl and the dough to keep it from sticking. Cover with a clean kitchen towel and leave to rise for an hour, until doubled in size.

Prepare the dough: Divide the dough into four portions on a floured surface, covering the portions you're not using yet to keep them from drying out.

Take a portion of the dough and roll it to a thickness of around 1.5cm (around ½ in), forming a circle roughly 30cm (12in) in diameter. Repeat the process with the remaining dough portions.

Spread each circle evenly with the chocolate spread, leaving a 5mm (¼in) rim. Sprinkle cinnamon evenly over each of these chocolate spread-covered circles. Now pick up the edges of each circle and gather together towards the middle, pressing the pastry together to seal the chocolate spread inside. Turn the filled dough over so that the pleated edge is underneath. Cover with a kitchen towel and leave to rise on the floured surface for 30 minutes.

Working on a floured surface, use a rolling pin roll to very gently flatten each dough parcel into a circle approximately 40–45cm (16–18in) around, so the dough is translucent and you can see the chocolate through it. Be careful not to break the dough.

Shape and bake the rugelach: Preheat the oven to 190°C/375°F. Line two baking trays with baking parchment.

Using a sharp knife, cut each round into 4 quarters. Then, cutting from the outside edge, cut each quarter into four wedges, forming 16 wedges in all.

Take one of the wedges and, working from the outer edge, pull and stretch the dough and roll up tightly. Place the tip underneath to hold it in place. Place on a lined baking tray. Repeat the process, spacing the rugelach well apart. Cover with a fine kitchen towel and leave to rise for 20 minutes.

Brush the risen rugelach with egg glaze and bake for 20 minutes, until golden brown.

Make the sugar syrup: Ten minutes before the rugelach are ready, simmer together the water, sugar and lemon juice over medium heat until the sugar has dissolved. Bring to the boil and cook for 5 minutes to form a light syrup. Remove from heat and set aside to cool slightly.

As soon as the rugelach are out of the oven, brush them generously 2–3 times with the warm syrup. Serve warm or at room temperature. They will keep for 5 days in an airtight container. Or you can freeze them in a tightly sealed container for up to 1 month.

This is a winning recipe! Rugelach are such a classic Jewish treat. I prefer to use margarine when making them, as I find the taste of butter too dominant. As the rugelach bake, they fill the house with the most inviting aroma. The rugelach themselves come out beautifully: golden brown, soft and filled with chocolate. They taste so good that no one believes they're not bought from a bakery! These are great fun to make with the children — quality time spent together. I don't know any child who doesn't enjoy a chocolate rugelach.

Shabbat
Shalom

SHABBAT

It's almost Shabbat (Shabbes), nearly time to light the candles, bless them as I do so, close my eyes and then, with tears, pray for each one of my kids, my family and myself, as my mother and grandmother did before me. I pray for those in my extended family who are sick, for the people in Israel and in the rest of the world. I pray for health, happiness and peace. When I finish my prayers, my children come to me in turn. I put my hands on their heads and bless them from my heart.

Keeping Shabbat is central to Judaism. It is an important holy day which marks the end of every week and sets up the next. Shabbat begins with the sunset on Friday night and ends on Saturday night with the appearance of the stars. Shabbat — which is a day of rest — symbolises the creation of the world; to observe it is a practical realistic acknowledgment of Genesis.

For Shabbat, I bake challahs and prepare dips, salads and special delicacies for the day, including rich cake for the morning. This is the time in our community that everything stops — work, phones and worries. Shabbat is a time for contemplation, a thoughtful period of rest and reflection.

CHALLAH

MAKES 3 LOAVES

YEAST MIXTURE

45g fresh yeast or 4½ tsp dried yeast

1 tsp sugar

1 tbsp flour

125ml (½ cup) lukewarm water

DOUGH

1.2kg (2lb 12oz) strong white bread flour

50g (4 tbsp) margarine, melted and cooled

100ml (3½ fl oz) sunflower oil, plus extra for coating

175g (⅞ cup) sugar

Around 700ml (2¾ cups) lukewarm water

1¼ tbsp salt

TOPPING

1 egg white beaten with a pinch each of sugar and salt, for glazing

Sesame seeds or poppy seeds (optional)

Prepare the yeast: Crumble the yeast into the bowl of a stand mixer or sprinkle in if using dried. Add the 1 tsp sugar, 1 tbsp flour and 125ml (½ cup) lukewarm water; stir gently. Cover with a clean towel and set aside for 15 minutes to become frothy.

Make the dough: Add the flour, margarine, oil and sugar to the yeast. Pour in half the lukewarm water and use the dough hook to mix at a low speed. As it mixes, gradually start to add in the remaining lukewarm water until you see the dough start to come away from the sides, bear in mind that you may need more or less water. Now, add the salt. Continue mixing for around 7 minutes, to form a soft, stretchy, slightly sticky dough.

Rise the dough: Coat the dough with oil. Cover with a clean kitchen towel and set it aside in a warm, dark place for 1 to 1½ hours until doubled in size. Break it down, knead briefly, cover and set aside to rise for 40 minutes to 1 hour, until doubled in size a second time.

"Nothing is more symbolic of Shabbat than challah. The evening meal and the early afternoon meal typically begin with a blessing called kiddush and another blessing recited over two loaves of challah."

Shape the challah loaves: Divide the dough into three even portions. Take one piece (covering the remaining dough up) and divide it into three even pieces. Working on a clean, lightly oiled surface, press the pieces flat with your hands. Roll each of them up and over to form a sausage shape, setting them aside to rest for a few minutes. Take one dough 'sausage' and roll it with your hands so that it becomes twice at long. Repeat the process with the remaining two sausage shapes, so you end up with three long strands.

Take the three long dough strands and pinch them together at one end. Now gently plait the strands together it is very important not to pull the dough. Tuck the ends underneath to neaten up the shape. Once the challah has formed, pat it gently along each side to even it up. Repeat the process with the remaining dough portions, making three challah loaves in all.

Rest the challah loaves: Cover the challah loaves with clean kitchen towels and set aside to rest and rise for 30 minutes.

Glaze and bake: Preheat the oven to 180°C/350°F. Brush each challah loaf generously with the egg glaze. Sprinkle neatly with pinches of sesame seeds or poppy seeds, if using. Bake for 25–30 minutes, until golden brown. Remove and cool on wire racks.

Nothing is more symbolic of Shabbat than challah. If you visit an Orthodox Jewish bakery on a Friday you will see dozens of freshly baked challah loaves on the shelves and hundreds of Hassidim trying to nab the best ones! It's an Ashkenazi tradition and my Sephardi family bought challah rather than making it, so I was thrilled to learn how to bake my own. In the Jewish Orthodox community making your own challah is a mitzvah (a duty) and part of the dough has to be set aside. I love making challah at home and my children also enjoy plaiting the dough. There is something deeply satisfying about seeing my family enjoy the soft, fresh challah that I have made for us.

קודש
שבת
לכבוד שבת קודש

SCHENNA – MOROCCAN CHAMIN

SERVES 6

MEATLOAF

300g (10oz) minced (chopped) beef
1 onion, finely grated and squeezed dry
1 courgette (zucchini), finely grated and squeezed dry
1 small potato, peeled, finely grated and squeezed dry
1 tbsp soy sauce
Salt and pepper
1 egg
2 tbsp matzo meal

THE SCHENNA

1 garlic bulb
750g (1lb 10oz) beef cuts, cut into large cubes*
400g (14oz) bone marrow*
3–4 medium potatoes, peeled
700g (1lb 8oz) dried chickpeas, soaked**
200g (1 cup) pearl barley or wheat grains
Water, to cover
6 hard-boiled eggs, shells on

FLAVOURING

3 tbsp oil
1 tsp coarse salt
1 tbsp sweet paprika
1 heaped tbsp chicken stock powder
2 tbsp honey
1 tbsp white sugar
1 tbsp Demerara (soft brown) sugar
125ml (½ cup) boiling water

Make the meatloaf: Place all ingredients in a mixing bowl and mix thoroughly with your hands. Shape the mixture into an oval cylinder roughly 13cm (5in) long.

Assemble the schenna: Trim the base of the garlic bulb, peel off the outer layer and cut incisions in the bulb to help release its flavour.

Place the meat pieces, bone marrow, meatloaf and garlic bulb in the base of a wide, deep pot. Top with the potatoes, chickpeas and barley. Pour over water to cover by 3cm (1¼in). Over a low heat, gradually bring to the boil.

Meanwhile, mix together all the flavouring ingredients in a small bowl.

Once the schenna has come to the boil, add the flavouring mixture. Reduce the heat, cover and cook over a low heat for 2 hours, until the chickpeas are tender and half the liquid has evaporated. If the chickpeas are not tender, add more hot water and cook until they are softened.

Now taste the schenna and add more salt if required. Add the hard-boiled eggs (with their shells on) and place the schenna on a hotplate overnight to cook slowly and gently, giving the dish a rich brown colour and a depth of flavour. Before serving, discard the garlic bulb and slice the meatloaf.

*The cuts I like to use are flanken, short rib and shin I also like to include a kosher beef cut called galabone, which is a bone from the knee. If using a galabone, use just 250g (9oz) of marrow bone. Layer the galabone with the meat in the base of the pot.

**Soak the chickpeas for at least 20 hours with 1 tsp bicarbonate, then drain and rinse. I often pre-soak a large quantity of chickpeas, then freeze them in batches so I have them ready to defrost and use.

As we are not allowed to cook on Shabbat, there is a Jewish tradition of slow-cooked dishes called Chamin that are prepared in advance and set to cook gently on a hotplate, then eaten for Shabbat day. Schenna is a Sephardi Chamin dish, in which, unlike the Ashkenazi Chamin dish called cholent, you can identity the separate ingredients. The slow-cooking gives the dish a rich brown colour and a caramelised sweetness.

VELVETY ORANGE CHICKEN

SERVES 6

12 chicken drumsticks

MARINADE

Freshly squeezed juice of 5 oranges
Zest of 1 orange
Zest of 1 lemon
125ml (½ cup) white wine (optional)
2 tbsp brown sugar
2 tbsp soy sauce
2 tbsp white vinegar
2 heaped tbsp apricot jam
½ tsp garlic powder
Salt and pepper
1 bay leaf
1 tbsp white sugar (optional)

TO THICKEN

1 tbsp cornflour
3 tbsp cold water

Whisk all the marinade ingredients together, apart from the white sugar, until well mixed. Taste the marinade and add the white sugar to sweeten if necessary.

Place the chicken drumsticks in a large dish. Pour the marinade over the chicken and rub it in. Cover and marinate in the fridge for at least 3 hours, ideally overnight.

Preheat the oven to 180°C/350°F.

Place the chicken drumsticks in a roasting pan. Pour over the marinade. Bake for 30–40 minutes, until cooked through and golden brown.

To thicken the sauce, transfer the roasting juices to a saucepan and bring to the boil. Mix the cornflour (corn starch) and cold water to a paste, add to the boiling juices while stirring and cook for 1 minute until thickened, stirring constantly to prevent lumps. Alternately, if you don't want to use cornflour, simply boil the roasting juices uncovered for 15–20 minutes until reduced and slightly thickened.

Serve the drumsticks with the sauce poured over.

This is one of the first dishes I learned to cook when I moved to London. We had friends coming for supper and, as I didn't know how to cook, I phoned my mum in a panic. She spent an hour on the phone taking me through the dish, step by step. The dinner party was a great success and I got a lot of compliments on my cooking! This dish fills the house with a lovely citrus fragrance, which always makes me think of home.

TAHINI DIP

MAKES 500ML (2 CUPS)

250ml (1 cup) tahini paste
Around 250ml (1 cup) cold water
Juice of 2 juicy lemons
4–5 garlic cloves, peeled and crushed
1 tsp salt
A good handful of finely chopped parsley (optional)

TIP: The best tahini is traditional, stone-ground tahini (rather than factory-made) which does not separate into oil and solids and has a better flavour.

Place the tahini paste in a mixing bowl. Using a whisk, slowly and gradually mix in the water, incorporating it well with each addition. At this stage, if making runny tahini dip (to use in pitta bread with falafel or sabich), add an extra 125ml (½ cup) cold water.

Add the lemon juice, garlic and salt. Whisk thoroughly until well mixed.

If adding parsley or coriander, simply fold it in with the whisk along with the lemon juice. Cover and chill until required.

FOR AN EASY OPTION

For a quick, easy version, place all the ingredients apart from the parsley in a mixing bowl and mix thoroughly using a hand blender. Add the parsley and mix in with a few short pulses.

In Israeli cooking, tahini dip is widely used. It's served with barbecued meats — chicken shishlik, Shawarma, kebab, grilled fish and falafel, to name but a few dishes. An essential accompaniment which is quick and easy to make and always part of a Shabbat meal.

In the 1970s, my family lived near a small Yemenite neighbourhood, Kerem Hateimanim, which had a simple but legendary barbecue restaurant called Tzarum, known for its juicy, tasty kebabs and succulent lamb shishlick. As soon as we sat down, an array of mezze dishes would appear on the Formica table-top before us: tahini dip, hummus, freshly grated tomatoes, finely chopped vegetable salads, zhoug, falafel, warm pitta bread, pickles and the most amazing chips (fries). Everything was cooked to perfection — Tzarum was famous for good reason. Shmuel Tzarum, the restaurant's owner, kindly gave my mum his recipe for tahini dip and this is how I make it to this day. His was the best barbecued food I've ever eaten. Sadly, he took his recipes to his grave. Whenever I cook kebabs on the barbecue for my parents, they say 'this is good, almost as good as Tzarum's'.

Halev Harachav (steak house),
Carmel Market

CHARRED CHILLIES

SERVES 8

10 long, hot red chillies
6–7 large, long, mild green chillies
2–3 garlic cloves, sliced
Salt
4 tbsp oil
2 tbsp vinegar

TIP: As you are handling chillies in this recipe, either wear gloves or be very careful to wash your hands thoroughly afterwards.

Place a metal mesh grill over the gas hob and preheat over high heat.

In batches, place chillies on the hot mesh grill and cook until blackened and blistered, turning with tongs. You want to cook the chillies until they are thoroughly charred on all sides.

Place the charred chillies in a plastic bag. Seal and set aside to steam until cool enough to handle.

Wearing plastic gloves, peel the skin off the chillies rinsing to remove any remaining flecks.

Thoroughly pat dry the rinsed chillies. Trim off the stem head and press out the seeds. Place in a bowl with garlic, sprinkle with salt and coat with oil and vinegar.

Serve with bread. They are also excellent with hummus.

TIP: If you don't have a gas hob, then char the chillies as above under a preheated grill/broiler.

My son David's desert island ingredient is chillies! He eats them with everything and when I make charred chillies he can devour the whole bowlful in 10 minutes! Eating that amount of chillies is not for the faint-hearted — that must be why he's so thin and strong.

UAK
טבק עוז

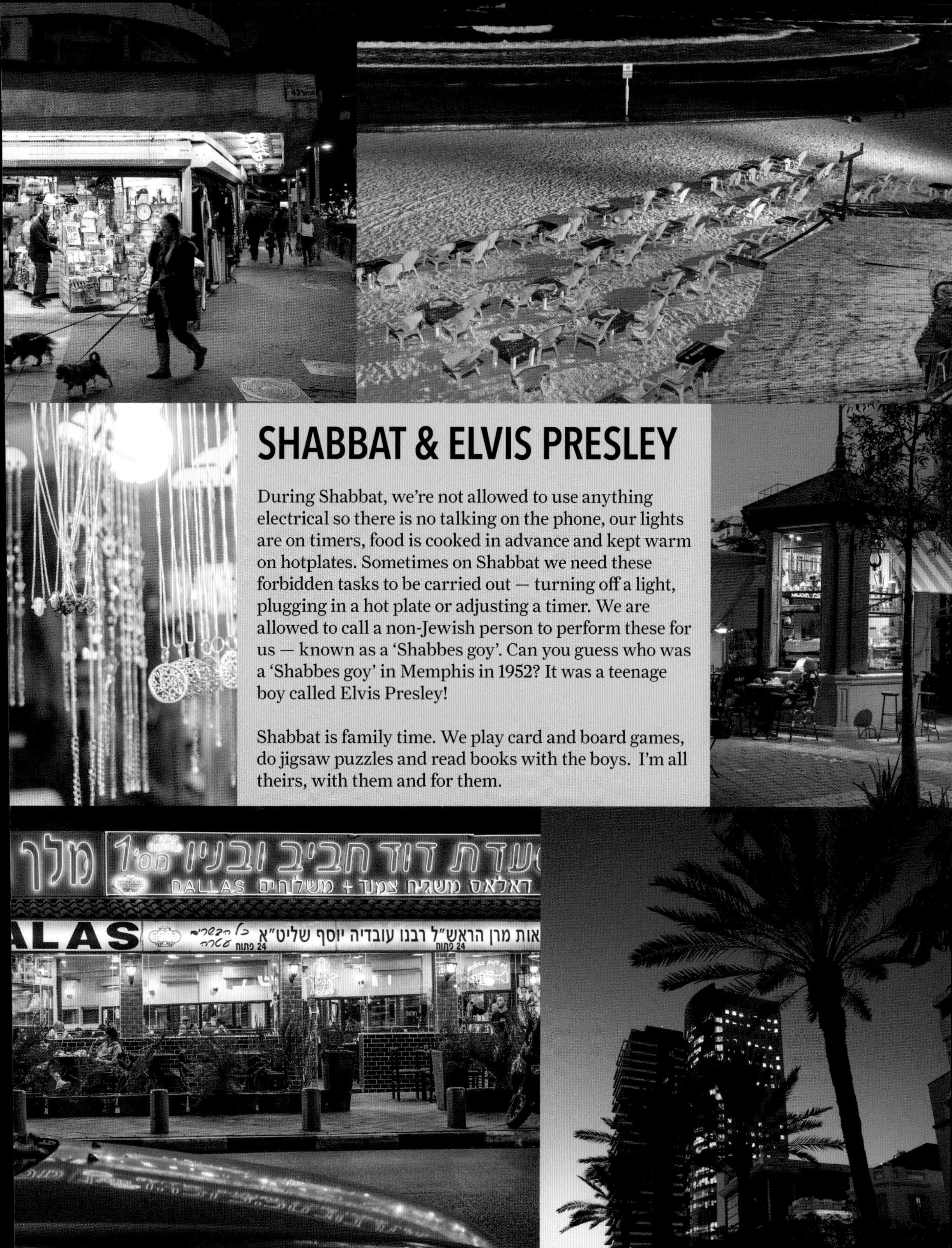

SHABBAT & ELVIS PRESLEY

During Shabbat, we're not allowed to use anything electrical so there is no talking on the phone, our lights are on timers, food is cooked in advance and kept warm on hotplates. Sometimes on Shabbat we need these forbidden tasks to be carried out — turning off a light, plugging in a hot plate or adjusting a timer. We are allowed to call a non-Jewish person to perform these for us — known as a 'Shabbes goy'. Can you guess who was a 'Shabbes goy' in Memphis in 1952? It was a teenage boy called Elvis Presley!

Shabbat is family time. We play card and board games, do jigsaw puzzles and read books with the boys. I'm all theirs, with them and for them.

MOROCCAN FISH

SERVES 6–8

8 skinless salmon fillets (each approximately 200g/7oz)*
Salt

SAUCE
3–4 large chillies
8 garlic cloves, peeled and halved
1–2 tomatoes, chopped
Handful of chopped coriander
250ml (1 cup) water

SPICED OIL
1 tbsp sweet paprika
1 tsp hot paprika
½ tsp turmeric
180ml (¾ cup) oil
½ tsp coarse salt

*I like to use a mixture of salmon and sea bass. I buy whole sea bass (1 large or 2 small) and ask for them to be gutted, then cut them across into 2–3 pieces, depending on the size of the fish. I also like to use the fish heads as they give extra flavour.

Salt the fish: Rinse and pat dry the fish. Place in a bowl, sprinkle a little salt over each piece, cover and chill for at least 3 hours or overnight.

Make the sauce: Cut a slit lengthways in the chillies. Spread the garlic cloves, tomatoes, chillies and coriander in an even layer in a large sauté pan.

Spice the fish: Mix together the spiced oil ingredients in a bowl. Dip each fish in the spiced oil coating on both sides, and place the coated fish in the pan. Pour over the remaining spiced oil and add the water.

Cook the fish: Over a medium heat, bring to a gentle simmer. Cover, reduce the heat to low and cook for 15 minutes. As it cooks, baste the fish with the sauce every now and then.

Uncover and cook for a further 5 minutes on a medium heat to thicken the sauce.

VARIATIONS

With chickpeas: add 600g (3 cups) of cooked chickpeas to the pan with the sauce ingredients, forming a layer beneath the fish, and an extra 250ml (1 cup) of water with 1 tsp chicken stock powder. Cover and cook for 25 minutes, then uncover and cook for 5 minutes more.

With potatoes: add 3–4 sliced potatoes to the layer underneath the fish, season with salt, and an extra 250ml of water. Cover and cook for 25 minutes, uncover and cook for 5 minutes more.

This is an authentic Moroccan fish recipe, requiring lots of bread to mop up the sauce with. Try it with the chickpeas or potatoes as above and you really will be licking your fingers!

BRAISED LAMB NECK

SERVES 6

3 tbsp oil
2 onions, sliced into thick rings
½ tsp ground turmeric
½ tsp sugar
Salt and pepper
1.5kg (3lb 6oz) neck of lamb slices
Freshly squeezed juice of 1 lemon
1–2 tbsp pine nuts, roasted, to garnish
Chopped parsley, to garnish

Heat the oil over medium heat in a large, shallow casserole dish. Add the onion and fry gently until softened. Sprinkle over the turmeric and sugar, season with salt and pepper, and mix well. Place the lamb slices in one layer over the onions

Cover, reduce heat to low and cook gently for 45 minutes. Turn the lamb slices over and cook for a further 45 minutes. Pour over the lemon juice and serve at once garnished with pine nuts and parsley. This goes well with Syrian Rice (see p.142).

"Sometimes less is more. Subtly spiced and slow-cooked, this simple dish of lamb in its own juices delivers a real depth of flavour that makes it a Shabbat treat."

POTATO KUGEL

SERVES 6

- 7 large baking potatoes, peeled, finely grated, and squeezed dry
- 6 eggs
- 185ml (6½ fl oz) sunflower oil
- 1 tsp sugar
- 1 tsp salt
- 1 large onion, coarsely grated and squeezed dry
- 2 tbsp fine matzo meal or potato flour

Preheat oven to 180°C/350°F and grease a 20cm (8in) springform round cake tin.

In a bowl, thoroughly mix all the ingredients with your hands.

Place the mixture in the greased cake tin, smooth the surface and bake for 30 minutes till golden. Serve hot or at room temperature.

Kugels are a much-loved staple of Ashkenazi cuisine and there are many versions: noodle, apple, courgette (zucchini) and, the most common, potato. When my kids started to go to Hassidic school, they asked me to make it for them. As a Sephardi Jew, I was not familiar with the dish. Traditionally, it is cooked for a long time on a hot plate until the inside turns grey — not an appetizing colour! In my version, the potato kugel is eaten fresh out of the oven, when the top is golden-brown and the inside soft and yellow. My kids say it's the best kugel they've ever eaten — smart kids!

SUCCULENT POT-ROAST

SERVES 8

- 1.5kg (3lb 6oz) piece of braising beef – the best cut is side bola (feather steak joint)
- Oil for frying
- 1 tbsp chicken stock powder
- Ground black pepper
- 1 tsp sugar

GRAVY

- 2 tbsp oil
- 1 small onion, finely chopped
- 1 garlic clove, crushed
- A pinch of turmeric
- Salt
- 1 tbsp cornflour (corn starch)
- 3 tbsp cold water
- A small handful chopped parsley, to serve (optional)

TIP: If making in advance, prepare the recipe to the sliced beef stage. Wrap the beef slices in baking parchment, then place in a plastic bag and freeze. Store the broth in a plastic container and freeze. When using, defrost both the beef and the broth and continue the recipe from the gravy stage.

Cook the beef: Pat the beef dry using kitchen paper. Heat oil for frying in a wide, deep pot over high heat. Add the beef, reduce the heat to medium and brown the meat on all sides.

Remove the beef, spoon out the oil and return the beef to the pot. Pour in enough water to barely cover the meat. Add stock powder, black pepper and sugar. Bring to the boil, skim, reduce the heat to very low, cover and cook for 1½ hours, turning the meat over halfway through.

Cool to room temperature, then chill the beef in its cooking liquid overnight.

The next day, take the beef out of the broth, reserving the liquid – you will need it for further cooking. Cut the beef into 1cm (around ⅓in) slices.

Make the gravy: Heat the oil in a large sauté pan over medium heat. Fry the onion until soft and translucent. Add the garlic and turmeric, mixing in, and pour in 1 litre of the reserved beef broth. Bring to the boil, then reduce the heat to medium and simmer. Taste and adjust the seasoning.

Mix the cornflour with the cold water, stirring well to ensure there are no lumps. Bring the gravy to the boil. Add the cornflour paste to the boiling gravy, stirring it as you do. Cook, stirring, for 1 minute. Add the beef slices to the pan, ensuring that they are covered by the gravy; if not, add more broth.

Return to the boil, reduce heat, cover and cook for 30 minutes until the sauce has thickened. Sprinkle with parsley, if using. Serve with German-style potatoes (see following page) or rice.

Even though there are more luxurious versions of pot-roast – using wine, shallots and various vegetables – for me this straightforward recipe, which I ate at a neighbour's house, is the best.

TZIMMES

SERVES 6

1kg (2lb 4oz) carrots, peeled and sliced, or frozen baby carrots
2 tbsp oil
1 heaped tbsp honey
1 tbsp Demerara (soft brown) sugar
2–3 tbsp white sugar
¼ tsp ground cinnamon (optional)
½ tsp salt
Pinch of black pepper
Juice ½ lemon
125ml (½ cup) water

Place all ingredients in a saucepan, cover and cook over a low heat for 20–30 minutes, stirring now and then until softened. Uncover and cook for a further 5 minutes on a medium heat, taste and adjust the seasoning.

TIP: for a festive version, add 120g (8oz) canned pineapple chunks in syrup, 125ml (½ cup) pineapple syrup, 10 pitted prunes and a handful of raisins.

Tzimmes is an excellent accompaniment to meat dishes, such as the Succulent Pot-Roast (p.202) or Braised Lamb Neck (p.199). Cooking vegetables in their own juices in this way — with no extra water — makes them very tasty. We also eat it as one of the symbolic dishes to celebrate the New Year.

GERMAN-STYLE POTATOES

SERVES 5–6

1.5kg (3lb 5oz) waxy potatoes, peeled
Coarse salt
3 tbsp oil
3–4 short strips of lamb fat
Coarsely ground black pepper
½ tsp sugar (optional)

Place the potatoes in a saucepan, cover with water, season with salt and bring to the boil. Reduce the heat, cover and cook over a low heat for 5 minutes until par-boiled. Drain, cool slightly and cut into chunks or slices.

Heat the oil with the lamb fat in a wide frying pan over a low heat until the lamb fat has turned golden brown and reduced in size. Increase the heat to medium, add the potatoes, and season with salt, pepper and sugar (if using). Fry for 20 minutes, stirring gently now and then, until the potatoes are golden. Remove the lamb fat and serve at once.

This ingenious cooking method delivers potatoes which are neither roasted nor French-fried but something in between, crisp on the outside and tender inside. Absolutely delicious!

APRICOT-GLAZED CHICKEN

SERVES 6

7 tbsp olive oil
2 tbsp apricot jam
1 garlic clove, crushed, or ½ tsp garlic powder
1 tsp honey
Juice of 1 lemon
Sea salt flakes
Ground black pepper
6 chicken legs
180ml (6½ fl oz) chicken stock
5 potatoes, peeled and quartered
2–3 sprigs of thyme

Preheat the oven to 180°C/350°F.

In a mixing bowl, mix the olive oil, jam, garlic, honey and lemon juice. Season with salt and pepper. Taste and adjust the seasoning.

Using your hands, smear the mixture all over the chicken legs, making sure to coat the skin well.

Place the chicken legs skin side up in a roasting tray. Place the potatoes in the bowl used for the marinade and mix to coat well with the remaining marinade. Tuck the potatoes between and under the chicken legs, reserving the marinade bowl.

Add the stock to the marinade bowl, scrape the sides, mix well and season with salt.
Pour this into the roasting tray around the chicken pieces. Dot with the thyme sprigs.

Bake for 50 minutes, until the chicken is cooked through.

I usually cook this for Shabbat or for Yom Kippur evening as it's a light dish, which is perfect before fasting. Though very easy, it looks impressive, making it a useful dish when you have to entertain at short notice.

The Milky Way

23

'Romia', Yemenite Falafel in Iben Gabirol, Tel Aviv

COTTAGE CHEESE AND TOMATO LASAGNE

SERVE 6–8

TOMATO SAUCE
40g (4 tbsp) butter
2 tbsp olive oil
3 garlic cloves, crushed
5 tbsp tomato paste
1 tsp dried oregano
180ml (¾ cup) water
Salt and pepper
1 tbsp sugar

CHEESE LAYER
500g (1lb 2oz) cottage cheese
2 eggs
2 tbsp crumbled feta cheese or sour cream
Salt and pepper (reduce salt if using feta)
8 basil leaves, chopped
100ml (3½ fl oz) whipping cream
10–12 slices mozzarella, Port Salut or Havarti cheese

250g (9oz) oven-ready lasagne sheets

TOPPING
6–8 pitted black olives
Basil leaves to garnish

Preheat the oven to 180°C/350°F. Butter a 20 x 35 (8 x 12in) baking dish.

Make tomato sauce: Heat the butter and olive oil in a saucepan over medium heat. Add the garlic and fry for under 1 minute to soften. Add the remaining ingredients and bring to the boil. Reduce the heat and cook for 2–3 minutes.

Make the cheese layer: Mix all the cheese layer ingredients, apart from the mozzarella slices.

Assemble the lasagne: Evenly spread 4 tbsp of the tomato sauce in the base of the baking dish. Top with a layer of lasagne sheets, then spoon over a third of the tomato sauce, then a third of cheese mixture. Layer with mozzarella slices. Repeat the process twice more. Top with the olives. Bake for 30 minutes until the cheese is bubbling. Garnish with basil and serve.

For kosher reasons — so as to avoid combining milk with meat — lasagne in Israel comes in two basic versions: one made with cheese and tomato sauce and the other with meat sauce but without cheese. I am not sure when lasagne first arrived in Israel, but I remember the first time I ate it in a coffee shop in the 1990s. Once we discovered a good recipe, my mother would make it for Shavuot. This version is for the traditional tomato with cottage cheese, which I love using. I remember fondly the cottage cheese tubs in Israel with their pictures of English cottages!

SMOKEY AUBERGINE CHEESE FRITTERS

MAKES 10–12

FRITTERS

3 large aubergines (eggplant)
100g (3½ oz) feta cheese, crumbled
50g (2oz) grated Emmental, kashkaval or other mild, firm cheese
1 garlic clove, crushed
1 egg, whisked
2 tbsp potato flour
2 tbsp matzo meal
Salt and pepper

FOR FRYING

4 tbsp oil

SERVING DIP

250g (9oz) sour cream
4 spring onions (scallions), finely chopped, or a bunch of chives, finely chopped
1 level tsp onion soup mix

Char the aubergines (eggplant) until blackened on all sides and softened (see tip). Place in a colander to cool and drain.

Peel off the charred skin and trim and discard stems. Place the flesh in a colander and squeeze out excess moisture. Chop the flesh. Place in a bowl and add other ingredients, mixing together well with a fork; the mixture should be firm-ish and able to hold together.

Heat the oil in a frying pan over medium heat. Take a tbsp of the mixture and form into a round flat fritter, using oiled hands or two spoons. Add it to the hot oil and repeat the process. Fry the fritters in batches for 1–2 minutes on each side till golden; drain on kitchen paper and keep warm until serving.

Mix the dip ingredients. Serve the dip on the side.

TIP: Choose aubergines (eggplant) that are light in weight and smooth and shiny. To do the charring, I place a wire rack on the stove, then put the aubergine (eggplant) — as is or wrapped in foil — on top of the rack. Once the underneath has softened, I turn it carefully using tongs. Care must be taken not to pierce the aubergines during the charring process.

These are my gourmet fritters. I usually make them for Passover or, as they contain cheese, for Shavuot when it is traditional to eat dairy products. Charring the skin gives a smoky taste and adds a sophisticated depth of flavour. Put them on the table and they will disappear fast!

BAKERY SAID ABUEL

Abuelafia Bakery, Jaffa

BOREKITAS – CHEESE PASTRIES

MAKES AROUND 40

PASTRY

400g (3 cups) flour

200g (⅞ cup) butter at room temperature, cubed

250g (9oz) soft white cheese, such as Quark

1 tsp salt

FILLING

250g (9oz) Bulgarian or feta cheese, crumbled

150g (5oz) Emmental cheese, grated

100g (3½ oz) soft white cheese, such as Quark

Salt and paper

1 egg

1 heaped tbsp potato flour

GLAZE

1 egg beaten

Sesame seeds

Place all pastry ingredients in a stand mixer. Using the K-paddle, mix at medium speed until they come together to form a soft pastry. Cover the pastry with a clean kitchen towel and leave to rest in a cool place for an hour.

Make the filling by mixing all the ingredients well.

Heat the oven to 180°C/350°F. Line two baking trays with baking parchment.

Roll out the pastry on a floured surface to a thickness of around 4–5mm (around ⅕ in). Using a 10cm (4in) circular cutter, cut out circles from the pastry. Place a teaspoon of filling in the centre of each circle, fold over the pastry and press together to seal well.

Place the borekitas on the trays, spacing them well apart. Brush with beaten egg and sprinkle with sesame seeds. Bake for 25 minutes until golden. Serve hot, warm or at room temperature.

“These small Turkish pastries are addictive! I always make two batches as they disappear so fast.”

γυρισμός GIRISMOS
ΣΤΕΛΙΟΣ ΚΑ
MINOS
FEDERAL RESERVE NOTE
THE UNITED STATES OF AMERICA

GREEK SALAD

SERVES 5

- 2 ripe but firm tomatoes, cut into 1.5cm (around ½ in) cubes
- 3 slender, firm cucumbers, cut into 1.5cm (around ½ in) cubes
- 1 light green pepper, cut into 1.5cm (around ½ in) pieces
- ½ red onion, finely sliced
- ½ tbsp dried oregano or 1 tbsp fresh oregano leaves
- 3–4 tbsp olive oil
- 1–2 tbsp freshly squeezed lemon juice
- Salt and pepper
- 200–250g (8–9oz) feta or Bulgarian cheese, sliced
- 12–14 pitted Kalamata or black Tassos olives

Put everything apart from the cheese and olives in a serving bowl, and mix well. Season with salt and pepper, bearing in mind the saltiness of the feta. Top with the feta and the olives and serve.

Greek music reminds me of the 1970s and 1980s, when Aris San, Kazantzidis and Trifonas were stars of the music scene in Israel. Greek salad reminds me of the 1990s, when it starred on menus everywhere in Tel Aviv, from cafés to pubs. Ah, the good old days!

FROM RAGS TO RICHES & BACK

My dad used to listen to football (soccer) matches on the radio like men all over Israel. He used to buy his weekly Toto form (Football Pools) to participate in the national football lottery.

Every weekend my father was convinced that the games were going his way, checking his form as the radio crackled away. An hour before the end of all the matches, he used to tell us what would happen if he won. He would describe in great detail the private villa that we would have, with a large swimming pool and the luxurious American car we would drive. He would ask each child in turn to say what kind of toy they would like to buy. We imagined ourselves sitting happily in this enormous car or basking in the sun next to the swimming pool and playing with our new toys. As the games ended and we realised that he hadn't won, the dreams faded. We were back again in our flat, with our old car, yet happy!

מאנה
MANNE
3005

BEETROOT AND WARM GOAT'S CHEESE SALAD

SERVES 4

3 medium beetroot (beets), peeled
5 tbsp oil
Flour for coating
Salt and pepper
2 eggs
Panko breadcrumbs for coating
16 slices of goat's cheese, 5mm (around ¼in) thick, cut from a log or crottins
100g (3½ oz) rocket leaves
50g (2oz) toasted pine nuts

DRESSING

125ml (½ cup) olive oil
Juice of ½ orange
1 tbsp lemon juice
1 tbsp red wine vinegar
1 tsp balsamic vinegar
1 garlic clove, crushed
1–2 tsp honey

Place the beetroot (beet) in a saucepan and cover with water. Bring to the boil, cover, reduce the heat and cook for 30 minutes, until just tender but retaining their texture. Transfer to cold water to stop the cooking process, remove and pat dry. Trim and cut the beetroot (beet), so that you have 16 slices overall.

Place the dressing ingredients in a lidded jar, close and shake well to mix.

Heat the oil in a frying pan over medium heat. Put flour for coating in a bowl and season with salt and pepper. Whisk eggs in a separate bowl. Flour each slice of cheese on both sides, dip in beaten egg then coat in panko breadcrumbs. Fry in the hot oil until golden. Remove and drain on kitchen paper.

For each serving, overlap 4 beetroot (beet) slices on a serving plate. Top with a handful of rocket and then 4 slices of the goat's cheese. Sprinkle with pine nuts, then spoon over 2–3 tbsp of the dressing. Serve at once.

> "This beautiful dish can be served as a starter or a meal in its own right. Food for the heart and soul."

SHAVUOT CHEESE BLINTZES

MAKES AROUND 16 BLINTZES

140g (1 cup) flour
Pinch of salt
1 heaped tbsp sugar
50g (4 tbsp) butter
4 eggs
375ml (1½ cups) milk
1 tsp vanilla essence

FILLING*
500g (1lb 2oz) soft white cheese or cream cheese
5 tbsp sugar
Fresh chopped strawberries or raisins

Icing sugar, to serve

*alternatively see Rich Blintz Filling p.391

Make the blintzes: Place the flour, salt and sugar in the bowl of a stand mixer and stir with a spoon.

Melt the butter over a low heat in a small pan and set aside to cool slightly.

In a separate bowl, using a hand whisk, beat together the eggs, milk and vanilla essence. Gradually, whisk in the melted butter.

Add the egg mixture to the flour mixture. Using the whisk attachment, whisk at high speed for 1 minute. If slightly lumpy, pass the batter through a sieve.

Heat a buttered 22cm (9in) blintz pan over medium-low heat. Stir the batter well and pour in a small ladleful of batter, tilting the pan to spread it thinly. Fry until it starts browning at the edges. Use a spatula to turn the blintz and fry it briefly for 10 seconds. Remove to a wooden board. Repeat the process, including the stirring, until all the batter has been used. Let the blintzes cool to room temperature.

Fill the blintzes: Mix the filling ingredients. Take a blintz, dark side up, and place a heaped tbsp of the filling on one side of the blintz. Fold a flap of the blintz over the filling, then fold over the sides and roll to form a neat parcel. Repeat the process.

Sprinkle the blintzes with sieved icing sugar and serve.

Shavuot is a festival to celebrate the giving of the Torah — but personally, what I always look forward to is these delicious blintzes! Adding melted butter to the batter is a fool-proof way of making even the first blintz work.

Balabuste in the Kitchen

'Balabuste' is a Yiddish term for a good homemaker. A powerful, capable woman who runs the house brilliantly and efficiently. Nothing is a challenge for her.

IRAQI BEETROOT KUBEH SOUP

SERVES: 6–8

KUBEH FILLING

1–2 tbsp oil
1 large onion, finely chopped
A pinch of sugar
2 tbsp golden raisins, soaked (optional)
300g (10oz) minced (chopped) beef
150g (5oz) minced (chopped] lamb
½ tsp baharat
Salt and pepper
125ml (½ cup) stock or water
2 tbsp celery leaves, finely chopped

SOUP

3 large beetroot (beets), peeled, washed and chopped into small chunks
7 tbsp sugar
Salt and pepper
3.5 litres (3½ quarts) chicken stock
2 tbsp tomato purée
1 celery stalk with leaves, chopped
½ tsp baharat or ground cinnamon
1 tbsp oil
Grated zest of 2 large unwaxed lemons
4–5 dried apricots (optional)

KUBEH DOUGH

600g (1lb 5oz) course semolina
1 tsp salt
1 tbsp sunflower oil
375ml (1½ cup) cold water

A squeeze of lemon juice, to serve

Prepare the filling: Heat the oil in a frying pan. Add the onion, sprinkle over the sugar and fry gently over a low heat, stirring often, until lightly golden and caramelized, around 15–20 minutes.

Drain the raisins, if using, and mix in. Fry for 2 minutes. Add the beef and lamb and fry, stirring with a fork to break up the lumps. Keep frying, stirring now and then, until the meat loses its raw red colour.

Season with baharat, salt and pepper, and mix in the stock. Cover and cook the meat for around 30 minutes, stirring now and then. The meat should be soft, with no excess moisture left. Set aside to cool. Add the celery leaf and mix well by hand. Refrigerate for 3–4 hours

Make the soup: Put all the ingredients in a saucepan and bring to the boil. Cover, reduce heat and cook for half an hour or until the beetroot starts to soften. Taste and season accordingly. The taste should be sweet and sour.

Make the dough: Place the semolina, salt and oil in a bowl. Pour in the cold water and use your hands to gently and briefly stir it into the semolina; do not over-mix. You should see little puddles of water form on the surface. Cover with a clean kitchen towel and set aside to rest for 25 minutes, during which time the semolina will absorb the water, forming a dough.

Shape the meat filling for the kubeh: While the dough is resting, shape the chilled meat into small meatballs around 2cm (¾in) across. Place them on an oiled tray and partly freeze them for 10–15 minutes, until the dough is ready. This partial freezing of the meatballs makes it much easier to shape the kubeh.

Make the kubeh: With wet hands, shape the dough into ping pong-sized balls (each around 25g/1oz), placing on a tray as you do. Take one of the dough balls in your hands and gently pat it out to form a flat circle. Keeping it in the palm of your hand, place a meatball in the centre, then bring the dough circle up around the filling. Carefully pinch the edges together, sealing well. Roll and pat the kubeh in your hands to further seal it and shape into a ball. Repeat the process until all the meatballs have been used.

Cook the kubeh in the soup: Bring the soup to the boil and drop the kubeh into it as you form them. Reduce the heat, cover and simmer for 20–25 minutes until the kubeh are cooked through; they will rise to surface when they are done. Be careful not to overcook the kubeh as this makes the dough tough. Serve at once with a squeeze of lemon juice.

TIP: The traditional recipes uses ½ tsp lemon salt in the soup. I prefer to flavour the soup with lemon zest and to add the lemon juice at the end, that way it keeps the wonderful, deep purple-red colour!

In Middle Eastern cuisine, making kubeh is regarded as a skill that truly tests the ability of the cook. My Mum always said that if you can make kubeh well, you can cook anything!

With these kubeh, I look for three things which signify that they've been well-made: the dough casing should be thin, the kubeh should be soft, and there should be no gap between the dough and the filling.

Dark red in colour, with jewel-like globes floating in a sour-sweet liquid, this is the tastiest and most beautiful soup in the world!

MAIN MEALS
MIXED GRILL
SHAWERMA
SCHNITZEL
FALAFEL
KEBAB
CHICKEN STEAK
FRENCH FRIES
SALADS
HUMMUS
GREEK SALAD
ARABIC SALAD
CHICKEN SALAD
TUNA SALAD

STUFFED CHICKEN BREAST FOR TU BISHVAT

SERVES 4

4 chicken breast fillets, each around 350g (12oz)
Salt and pepper
3 eggs
1 tbsp mustard
1 tbsp mayonnaise
Panko crumbs, for coating
2 tbsp sesame seeds (optional)

FILLING
2–3 tbsp golden raisins
100g (3½ oz) dried apricots, chopped
5 tbsp red wine
5 tbsp oil
1 large onion, finely chopped
2 tsp sugar
¼ tsp baharat
Salt and pepper

2 tbsp oil

Make the filling: Soak the raisins and apricots in the red wine for 10–15 minutes.

Heat the oil in a frying pan over medium heat. Fry the onion with the sugar, stirring, for 10 minutes until the onion is caramelised. Add the wine-soaked raisins and apricots and cook, stirring, until the wine has been cooked off. Add the baharat and season with salt and pepper. Mix and set aside to cool.

Using a meat mallet, flatten each chicken breast between two sheets of plastic, (taking care not to tear the flesh), to around 5mm (¼in) thick.

Place 2–3 tbsp of the filling along the bottom length of chicken breast. Roll the chicken up over the filling, making sure it is contained, and trim off excess chicken. Repeat with the remaining breasts.

Wrap each filled chicken breast tightly in cling film, twisting the ends of each parcel to keep it tightly wrapped. Freeze the parcels for 30 minutes to firm them up.

Prepare the coating: Preheat the oven to 180°C/350°F. Line an oven tray with a baking sheet and lightly coat with the oil.

Beat the eggs with the mustard, mayonnaise, salt and pepper in a wide, shallow bowl. Fill a separate wide bowl with panko crumbs and sesame seeds (if using).

Bake the chicken parcels: Unwrap the chicken parcels and coat them in the beaten egg mixture, then with the panko crumbs, shaking off excess.

Transfer the parcels to the oiled baking sheet and bake for approx. 40 minutes until golden. Slice across diagonally and for each portion serve a few slices of the chicken parcel with mashed potato.

This elegant celebratory dish is one I always make for Tu Bishvat. It's a recipe which transforms a schnitzel base into a filled parcel, offering a delicious surprise with every bite.

Jerusalem

MEAT KREPLACH

MAKES 50–60 KREPLACH

FILLING
2–3 tbsp oil
1 large onion, finely chopped
500g (1lb 2oz) minced (chopped) beef
Salt and pepper
Pinch of turmeric powder
125ml (½ cup) chicken stock

DOUGH
250g (1¾ cups) flour
250g (1¾ cups) strong flour
2 eggs and 2 yolks
1–2 tbsp oil
2 tsp salt
125ml (½ cup) water

TIP: When making kreplach, bear in mind that the filling needs to be prepared a day ahead so that it can rest and chill.

Make the filling: Heat the oil in a frying pan over medium-low heat. Add the onion and fry, stirring now and then, until golden.

Add the minced beef and fry, mashing with a fork and mixing it with the onion until the meat loses its raw colour. Season with salt, pepper and the turmeric and add the stock, mixing well.

Cover and cook over low heat, stirring now and then, until all the stock is absorbed. Using a hand blender, briefly mince most of the mixture to make it finer. Set aside to cool, then cover and refrigerate overnight.

The following day, make the dough: Place the two types of flour, salt, eggs, yolks and oil in the bowl of a stand mixer. Using the K-paddle, mix the ingredients together. Gradually add the water, mixing to form a soft, supple dough. Cover the bowl with cling film and rest for 30 minutes at room temperature.

Shape the meatballs: Shape the meat into small 2cm (around ¾ in) meatballs.

Roll out the dough: Divide the dough into two pieces. Cover the half you're not using with a clean kitchen towel to keep it from drying out. Using a long, thin roller, roll out half the dough very finely on a lightly floured surface to a thickness of 2mm (around 1⁄16 in), turning the dough over as you roll it out. Repeat the process with the remaining dough. Alternately, pass the dough through a pasta machine until it is 2mm (around 1⁄16 in) thick.

Make the kreplach {see photos}: Place one of the sheets on a work surface, leaving the other one covered. Place the meatballs on the dough sheet, leaving 3cm (1¼ in) spaces between. Carefully top with the other dough sheet. Using a 4.5cm (around 1¾ in) circular ravioli cutter, press down around each meatball and twist to form a round kreplach.

Cook the kreplach: Bring a large saucepan of salted water to the boil (I like to do this while I am making the kreplach in order to have it ready). Cook the kreplach in batches in the water for 5–6 minutes, until they float to the surface. Remove carefully with a slotted spoon, drain well and allow to cool. If using on the same day, chill until needed.

If freezing at this stage, layer the cooled kreplach in a freezer-proof container, separating each layer with baking parchment.

Add the kreplach to chicken soup: Kreplach are eaten in chicken soup (see recipe p.52). Add the cooked kreplach to the hot soup in the pan, bring the soup to the boil and cook for 2 minutes to heat through. Allow a few kreplach for each serving.

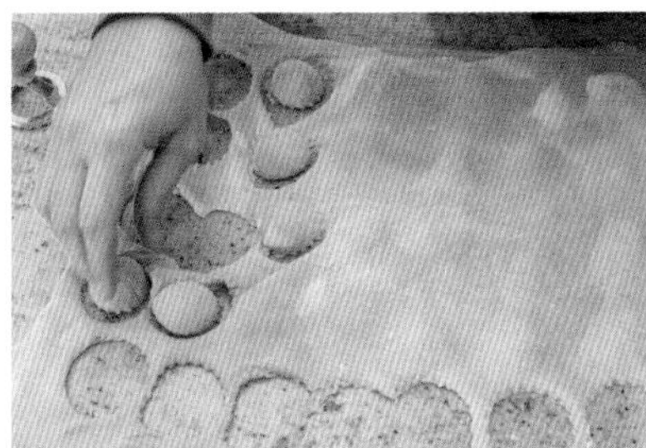

In the Hassidic community, stuffed foods like meat kreplach symbolize God's forgiveness and are traditionally eaten before Yom Kippur, Hoshana Rabbah and Purim. I always enjoy making kreplach with my kids. My son Yoeli has become expert at cutting them out with a ravioli cutter. Not only are kreplach symbolic, they are also truly delicious!

Western Wall, Jerusalem

STUFFED VINE LEAVES

MAKES 25 STUFFED VINE LEAVES

Around 30 large vine leaves in brine, washed thoroughly to rinse off excess salt

FILLING

200g (1 cup) basmati rice

300ml (10 fl oz) boiling vegetable or chicken stock

4 tbsp olive oil

2 tbsp sunflower oil

1 onion, finely chopped

1 red onion, finely chopped

100g (3½ oz) dried apricots chopped

100g (3½ oz) of a mixture of golden and black raisins

2 garlic cloves, crushed

2 tbsp toasted pine nuts (optional)

2 tbsp chopped dill

½ tbsp dried mint

A pinch of baharat

Salt and pepper

SAUCE

2 tbsp oil

2–3 lemon slices

2–3 tbsp pomegranate molasses

Juice and grated zest of 1 lemon

¼ tsp baharat

Salt and pepper

1 level tsp dried mint

1–2 tbsp sugar

Hot water to cover

Lemon wedges, to serve

Greek yogurt, to serve (optional)

Prepare the filling: Place the rice in a small pan, add the stock, mix and bring to boil. Cover, reduce heat and simmer for 5 minutes until the rice is almost cooked and the stock absorbed. Place in a large bowl.

Heat the two oils in a frying pan. Add the onions and fry over a medium-low heat, stirring now and then, until lightly golden. Add the apricots. raisins and garlic, mix in and fry for 1 minute. Add the onion mixture to the rice together with the remaining filling ingredients. Mix well. Taste and adjust the seasoning as required.

Stuff the vine leaves: Pat one vine leaf dry and place vein side up on a wooden surface. Spread the leaf out, with the base closest to you. Take 1–2 heaped tsp of the filling and shape it into a little cylinder. Place the filling on the leaf near the base. First, make one fold of the leaf tightly from the base over the filling, then fold the two sides over the filling and roll up tightly to form a neat, tightly-rolled, cigar-shaped parcel. Repeat the process until you have 25 stuffed vine leaves.

Cook the stuffed vine leaves: Place 2 tbsp oil in a wide sauté pan. Line the pan evenly with the remaining vine leaves, overlapping them in the pan, Neatly place the stuffed vine leaves, seam side-down, in a layer. It's important that the vine leaves fit snugly in the pan to prevent them opening. Top with the lemon slices.

Mix the remaining sauce ingredients and pour over the vine leaves. Place a heavy heatproof plate on top to weigh the vine leaves down. Pour in hot water until it just reaches the plate. Cover the pan, bring to the boil, reduce the heat and cook for 30 minutes, until all the sauce has practically gone (lift the plate to check its progress). Serve the stuffed vine leaves hot, at room temperature or cold.

Stuffed vine leaves are found throughout the Middle East: Turkish dolmeh, Kurdish Yaffrach, Lebanese Yabrak, Syrian Yabrah, Balkan Saramella and Palestinian Dwali. The filling is usually made from round rice, but my family use long grain rice. My grandmother Zohara had a beautiful large vine in her garden which bore the sweetest grapes I've ever tasted. As children we would be sent out to pick the young, tender vine leaves, which she and my mother would then use to make this dish.

TANZIA

SERVES 6

FOR THE LAMB
2 litres (8 cups) water
1 tbsp chicken stock powder
2 bay leaves
1 onion, halved
1 tsp turmeric
1 tsp allspice berries, crushed
1.5–2kg boneless rack of lamb

DRIED FRUIT MIXTURE
60g (2oz) raisins
250ml sweet red kiddush wine
Oil for frying
3 onions, halved and sliced
1 tbsp sugar
1 tbsp honey
100g (3½ oz) dried apricots
100g (3½ oz) prunes

SEASONING
1 allspice berry, crushed
1 tsp ground cinnamon
Pinch of grated nutmeg
Pinch of turmeric
1 tbsp chicken stock powder
Salt and pepper

60g (2oz) flaked roasted almonds or chopped roasted nuts
Juice of 1 lemon

TIP: If you can't find kiddush wine, use red wine instead. Taste and sweeten with sugar.

Cook the lamb: Place all the ingredients, apart from the lamb, in a large pot. Bring to the boil, add the lamb and return to the boil. Reduce the heat, cover and cook for 1 hour until tender. Drain the meat (reserving the stock for future use if desired) and set aside until cool enough to handle.

Cook the dried fruit: Place the raisins in a small bowl, cover with a little of the red wine and set aside for 30 minutes; drain.

In the meantime, pour enough oil into a large saucepan to cover the surface thinly. Fry the onion for 30 minutes over a low heat, stirring often, until caramelised. Add the sugar, honey, apricots, prunes and raisins and fry over medium heat, stirring to coat the fruit. Add the seasoning ingredients, the remaining red wine and season with pepper. Reduce the heat and cook, uncovered, for 15 minutes. Taste to check the seasoning and adjust as required.

Shred the lamb and add it to the simmering fruit. Add the flaked almonds. Gently stir once and cook, uncovered, over low heat for 30 minutes, slightly tilting and gently shaking the pan now and then to mix it, until the sauce has reduced considerably.

Sprinkle over half the lemon juice and stir in gently so as not to break the fruit up. Taste and add more lemon juice if needed. Serve the tanzia warm on top of couscous.

Tanzia is a celebratory dish, eaten for special occasions such as Tu Bishvat. It combines caramelized dried fruit, cooked in sweet red wine, with melt-in-the-mouth lamb. When a Moroccan family cooks tanzia, the whole neighbourhood smells it! My personal touch is the addition of fresh lemon juice, which nicely cuts through the sweetness and richness of the dish.

מבצע
20=
מבצע
20=

DATES
מג'הול
20=
מבצע

KUBEH NABALSIYA

MAKES AROUND 25 KUBEH

FILLING
3 tbsp oil
1 large onion, finely chopped
350g (11oz) finely minced (chopped) beef steak
350g (11oz) finely minced (chopped) lamb
Salt and pepper
2–3 tbsp pine nuts, roasted

DOUGH
225g fine bulgur (gerish)
70g (½ cup) flour
70g (½ cup) fine matzo meal
1 tsp sweet paprika
½ tsp hot paprika
1 tbsp ground cumin or baharat
1 tsp salt
2 tbsp oil
Around 375ml (1½ cups) lukewarm water

Oil for deep frying

Soak the bulgur for the dough in water for 30 minutes, drain, cover and set aside for at least 4 hours or overnight to dry thoroughly.

Make the filling: Heat the oil in a frying pan over medium heat. Add the onion and fry, stirring now and then, until light golden. Add the beef and lamb. Mash and mix the meat with a fork until it loses its raw colour. Fry, stirring often, until the excess liquid has cooked off. Season with salt and pepper and mix in the pine nuts. Allow to cool, then chill in the fridge.

Make the dough: Place the soaked, dried bulgur and the remaining dough ingredients, apart from the water, in a mixing bowl. Using your hands, thoroughly mix together. Gradually add the lukewarm water to form a soft dough, with a texture resembling plasticine. With wet hands, shape the dough into ping pong-sized balls. Cover with a clean kitchen towel so that the dough balls don't dry out.

FREEZING TIP: Once formed, filled and dried, the kubeh can be frozen, then fried as needed. I defrost them only part-way (around 3 hours in the fridge) as they may fall apart if defrosted completely.

Make the kubeh {see photos}: Use your thumb to make a hollow in a ball of dough. Gently pinch sides up to make a fine, oval-shaped shell around 8cm (3¼ in) long from the dough.

Fill the hollow in the centre of the shell with 1–2 tsp of the filling. Pinch the edges of the dough together to seal well. Set aside on kitchen paper to dry for around 20 minutes, as this keeps the oil from spitting when fried. Repeat the process until all the dough balls have been shaped and filled.

Heat the oil in a deep frying pan over medium-high heat. Once the oil is hot, add a piece of carrot to keep the oil clean and fry just one kubeh first. As it fries, roll it over to ensure it browns evenly. Once browned on all sides, remove with a slotted spoon and drain on kitchen paper. Now fry the kubeh in batches of 5–6 in the hot oil. Serve warm.

My husband's mother is from Aleppo and the first time we met he asked me whether I could cook kubeh, as it's a Syrian dish which he loves. Of course, I replied confidently, even though I couldn't even make rice! After we married, it took 10 years of learning how to cook, before I ventured to try making kubeh. Amazingly, they turned out great the very first time — beautifully fried, plump and crisp. My husband was thrilled that his wife knew how to make kubeh well!

look
@
me

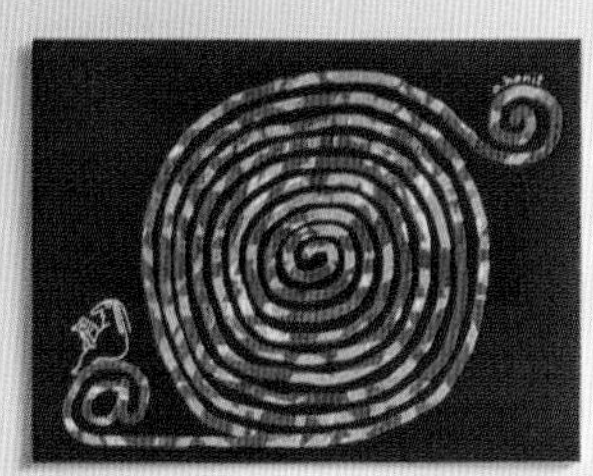

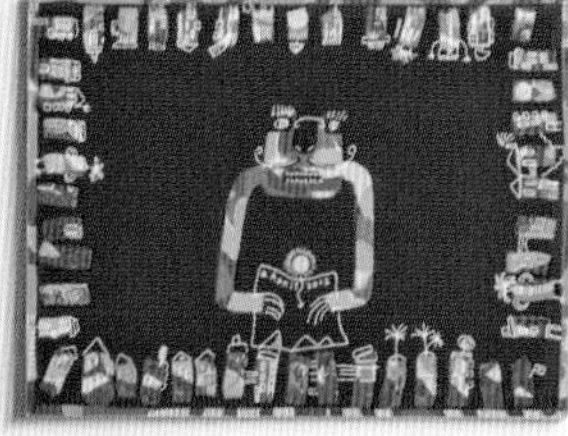

KEEP
SMILING

LAMB BUNS

MAKES 30

FILLING

2 tbsp olive oil

2 tbsp sunflower oil, plus extra for brushing

3 onions, sliced

500g (1lb 2oz) minced lamb (chopped)

200g (7oz) steak, roughly minced (chopped)

Salt and pepper

½ tsp turmeric

2 tbsp roasted pine nuts

DOUGH

25g fresh yeast or 2½ tsp of dried

1½ tbsp sugar

Lukewarm water, up to 250ml

500g (4 cups) white bread flour

100ml (3½ fl oz) olive oil

25g (2 tbsp) margarine, melted and lukewarm

1 heaped tsp salt

GLAZE

1 egg, beaten

1 tbsp oil

Poppy seeds

Make the filling: Heat both oils in a large frying pan over a low to medium heat. Gently fry the onion until golden brown, stirring often. Add the lamb and beef and increase the heat. Mash and mix the meat with a fork until it loses its raw colour. Season with salt, pepper and turmeric. Fry, stirring often, until the excess liquid has cooked off. Mix in the pine nuts and set aside to cool completely.

Make the dough: Crumble the yeast into the bowl of a stand mixer; if using dried, sprinkle in. Add ½ tbsp sugar, 100ml (3½ fl oz) lukewarm water and 1 tbsp of the flour; mix lightly with a spoon. Cover with a clean kitchen towel and set aside to rise for 15 minutes, during which time the mixture should become foamy.

Add the remaining flour to the yeast mixture along with the remaining sugar, olive oil and melted margarine. Using the dough hook in the stand mixer, mix for 3 minutes at a slow speed, gradually adding the remaining water until it starts to form a soft dough. Add the salt and mix for 5 more minutes to form a soft, supple dough; add more lukewarm water if needed.

Lightly brush a little oil over the dough, then cover and set aside in a warm place for 1 hour until doubled in size.

Form the buns: Working on an oiled surface, cut the dough into 30 equal pieces and shape into balls. Flatten each ball of dough into a circle, roughly 10cm/4in in diameter. Place 1 heaped tbsp of the filling in the centre. Bring up the dough over the meat, pressing the edges together to seal them well, and place the bun on your work surface with the sealed side down. Repeat the process until all the dough has been used. Place the buns, spaced well apart, on baking trays lined with baking parchment. Cover with a clean kitchen towel and set aside to rise for 30 minutes.

Bake the buns: Preheat the oven to 180°C/350°F. Make the glaze by beating together the egg and oil. Brush the buns with the glaze and top each bun with a pinch of poppy seeds. Bake the buns for 30 minutes until golden brown.

Once for a very special dinner party, I made 30 of these lamb buns and put the freshly baked buns to cool on the counter in the kitchen. I popped out to the shops for a few minutes and when I got back the guests had arrived and all the buns had gone!

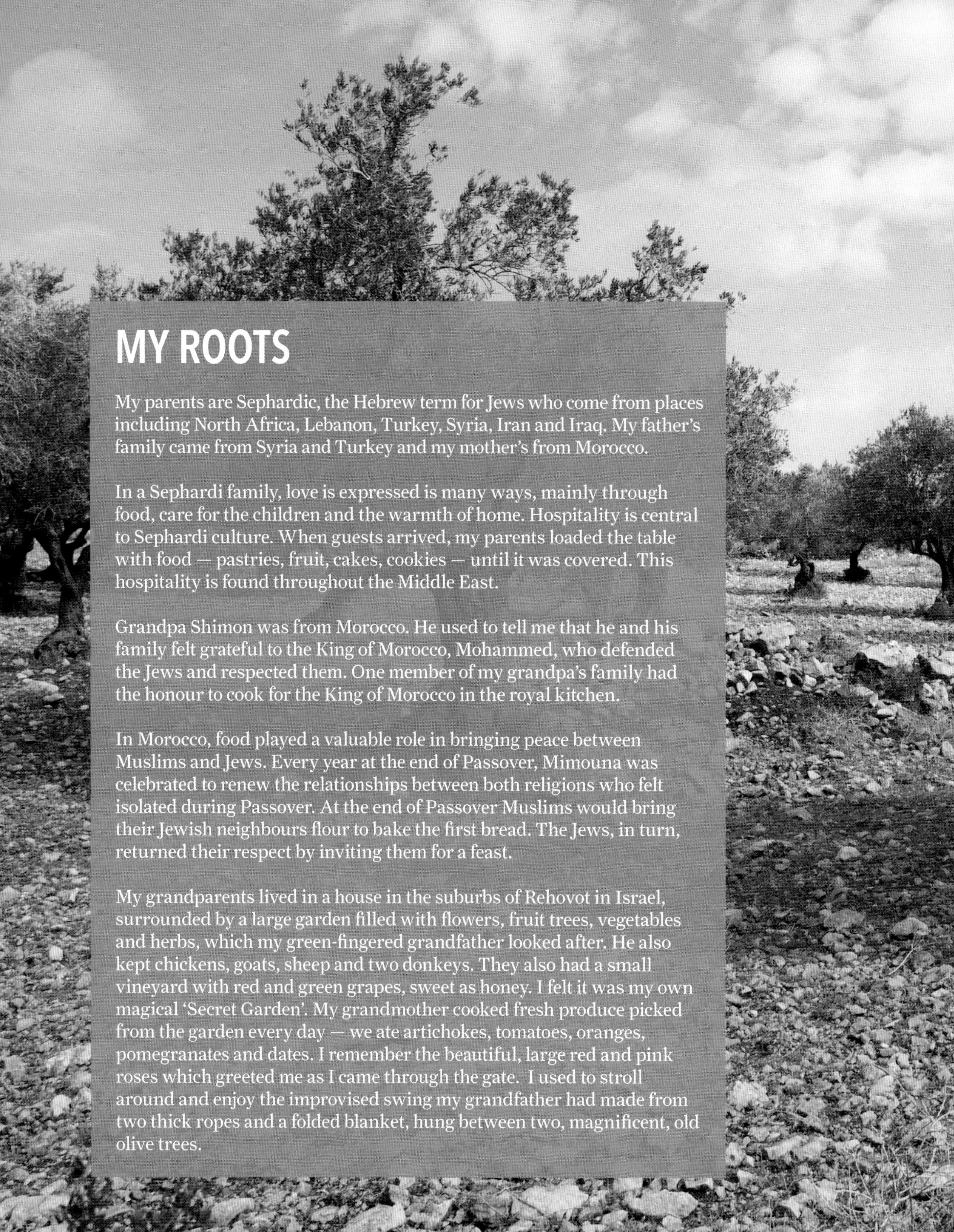

MY ROOTS

My parents are Sephardic, the Hebrew term for Jews who come from places including North Africa, Lebanon, Turkey, Syria, Iran and Iraq. My father's family came from Syria and Turkey and my mother's from Morocco.

In a Sephardi family, love is expressed is many ways, mainly through food, care for the children and the warmth of home. Hospitality is central to Sephardi culture. When guests arrived, my parents loaded the table with food — pastries, fruit, cakes, cookies — until it was covered. This hospitality is found throughout the Middle East.

Grandpa Shimon was from Morocco. He used to tell me that he and his family felt grateful to the King of Morocco, Mohammed, who defended the Jews and respected them. One member of my grandpa's family had the honour to cook for the King of Morocco in the royal kitchen.

In Morocco, food played a valuable role in bringing peace between Muslims and Jews. Every year at the end of Passover, Mimouna was celebrated to renew the relationships between both religions who felt isolated during Passover. At the end of Passover Muslims would bring their Jewish neighbours flour to bake the first bread. The Jews, in turn, returned their respect by inviting them for a feast.

My grandparents lived in a house in the suburbs of Rehovot in Israel, surrounded by a large garden filled with flowers, fruit trees, vegetables and herbs, which my green-fingered grandfather looked after. He also kept chickens, goats, sheep and two donkeys. They also had a small vineyard with red and green grapes, sweet as honey. I felt it was my own magical 'Secret Garden'. My grandmother cooked fresh produce picked from the garden every day — we ate artichokes, tomatoes, oranges, pomegranates and dates. I remember the beautiful, large red and pink roses which greeted me as I came through the gate. I used to stroll around and enjoy the improvised swing my grandfather had made from two thick ropes and a folded blanket, hung between two, magnificent, old olive trees.

GRANDMA ZOHARAH

If you don't have a Moroccan grandma then you have never experienced real hospitality! Grandma Zoharah was already waiting at the gate each time we visited, greeting us with warm expressions of affection, blessing, kissing and hugging us for at least half an hour. She sneaked a chocolate bar into the hands of each grandchild.

My Grandma was an amazing cook. She married young and taught herself how to cook. She made everything herself, from hand-rolled couscous to breads and preserved olives from their own olive trees. When I visited, she would make me various treats, including Moroccan doughnuts called 'sfinj', served coated with sugar. She used to make a special version of couscous with butter and sugar especially for me — I always had a sweet tooth. I was so full of energy that I craved sugar!

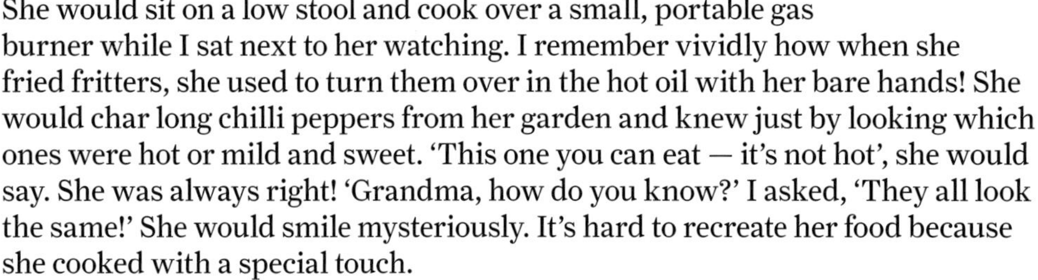

She would sit on a low stool and cook over a small, portable gas burner while I sat next to her watching. I remember vividly how when she fried fritters, she used to turn them over in the hot oil with her bare hands! She would char long chilli peppers from her garden and knew just by looking which ones were hot or mild and sweet. 'This one you can eat — it's not hot', she would say. She was always right! 'Grandma, how do you know?' I asked, 'They all look the same!' She would smile mysteriously. It's hard to recreate her food because she cooked with a special touch.

When I stayed at her house overnight, she would put me to sleep by patting me rhythmically on my shoulder, humming a Moroccan lullaby. When I woke up in the morning, she made me a cup of milky coffee, just like the grown-ups. She was the only person in my family who let me drink coffee as a child. She gave me money to go to the grocery store to buy any ice cream I wanted, as long as I finished my breakfast.

She was a profoundly devout woman in an innocent way. If she even saw a photo of a non-Kosher animal she would fast afterwards for 24 hours. After she died, we discovered that she did a lot of good works, but quietly, without anyone knowing. She would give her own food away to others in need. She never complained, even when she was unwell. She welcomed every visitor to her house with impeccable hospitality.

I miss her so much that it hurts.

GRANDPA SHIMON

Grandpa Shimon was remarkable. He reminded me of the Jewish character of Sallah Shabati from the famous Israeli film or the figure of a Juha in Muslim folklore — a shrewd farmer who, despite his innocence, knows how to make his way in the world.

My grandfather didn't have a car so he used a donkey and cart. During the summer holidays I used to keep him company when he went to work the fields, about 15 minutes away from their house. One day Grandpa left me in the cart while he went into the field. He told me to wait but I felt restless. I couldn't resist saying the special word 'barrr' which he used to get his donkey to move. The donkey leapt forward and started to run! 'Grandpa, help!' I called out, terrified. Grandpa Shimon rushed out of the field to chase down the runaway cart. He managed to catch up with us, seized the reins and stopped the donkey. 'If I haven't died now, I never will!"he told my mum later. He lived to be 100 years old.

My family has many more stories about Grandpa Shimon. Once when he lived in Morocco, he spent hours looking for his donkey before realizing that he was riding it. True story!

When Grandpa Shimon realised that his precious donkey tended to stray to the right while pulling the cart, he put an eye-patch over the donkey's right eye. People laughed at him for doing this. Funnily enough, the donkey walked straight from then on.

Another favourite story is when Grandpa Shimon went to comfort a recently bereaved family. When he got to their building, he simply entered the first flat with an open door, found a chair and sat down. The family who lived there looked at him strangely but said nothing. They thought he was a little odd, an old man who needed to rest. Grandpa sat there patiently for an hour before he realised that something wasn't quite right. He asked if they had lost someone. 'Ah, no, that's the family that live upstairs', they said.

TWO-STAGE HAND-ROLLED COUSCOUS

SERVES 8

1kg (2lb 4oz) coarse semolina
625ml (2½ cups) water
4 tbsp oil
½ tbsp salt

STAGE 1

Place the semolina in a large, deep, wide bowl. Flick in 250ml (1 cup) water using the fingertips of one hand, gradually sprinkling it in, while using a whisk in your other hand to whisk the semolina briskly. As you do this, the semolina comes together, forming little pearls of couscous.

Transfer the couscous to a couscous sieve. Holding it over the bowl, move the couscous with one hand in a circular motion and push it gently through the sieve, breaking up any clumps by passing them through the mesh.

Now prepare a couscousier or steamer. Fill the bottom section generously with water and cover with the lidded top section. Heat the couscousier so that the water comes to the boil.

Place the sifted semolina in the top part of the steamer. Use a fork to lightly aerate (fluff up) the couscous, creating a few steam holes in it.

Cover the couscous and steam over a medium-high heat for 20 minutes. Aerate with a fork every 5 minutes and make new steam holes to ensure even cooking. In the meantime, clean the bowl in which you made the couscous.

STAGE 2

Mix the remaining water with the oil and salt.

Return the couscous to the bowl. Use a whisk to stir the couscous and gently break up any lumps.

While whisking the couscous, gradually add the water mixture, whisking well between each addition. Leave to rest uncovered for 10 minutes.

If needed, top up the water in the bottom part of the steamer. Bring the water to the boil. Transfer the couscous to the top part of the steamer and aerate gently with a fork, making steam holes. Steam once again for 20 minutes, aerating with a fork and making steam holes every 5 minutes.

Transfer the couscous to a large bowl and whisk lightly to break down any lumps. Place in a serving bowl and serve.

Serving suggestion: Serve with couscous soup, see recipe in Basics (see p.384).

Note: If you are pushed for time see the recipe for Quick Couscous on p.385.

I have wonderfully vivid childhood memories of my Grandma Zohara sitting cross-legged on the ground in her courtyard sieving couscous. She had a very large couscous sieve and would toss the grains high into the air and catch them again. I can testify that not one grain fell to the ground! As she worked, she would smile at me, making it look so easy and effortless. When I ate the couscous she made for me, moistened with soup so as to make it soft and flavourful, I could taste her love for me. I can't make couscous in the same skilful way my late Grandma did, but this dish always reminds me of her and this recipe is written in her honour.

MOROCCAN MAFROUM

SERVES 5–6

6 medium potatoes
1 tbsp salt

FILLING
500g (1lb 2oz) minced (chopped) beef or lamb (or a 50/50 mixture of the two meats)
1 onion, finely chopped
1 garlic clove, finely chopped
A generous handful chopped celery leaves
1 egg yolk (reserve egg white for frying)
1 heaped tsp tomato paste
Salt and pepper
2 tbsp breadcrumbs

FOR FRYING
140g (1 cup) flour
1 egg plus the reserved 1 egg white
1 tsp tomato paste
Salt
Oil for frying

SAUCE
1 large onion, halved, finely sliced
6 garlic cloves. sliced
Half a celeriac, peeled and finely sliced
A handful of celery leaves, roughly chopped
2 carrots, finely sliced
Salt and pepper
1 tbsp tomato paste mixed with 125ml (½ cup) water

Prepare the potatoes: Peel the potatoes, cut off the curved ends, and slice them 1.5cm (around ½ in) thick. Slice each piece carefully across in the middle, but not all the way through, so that the two halves are still attached. Place the pieces in a bowl of cold water with 1 tbsp salt and set aside for an hour to soften, then drain.

Form the mafroum {see photos}: Thoroughly mix the filling ingredients and shape into ping pong-sized balls. Use each ball to fill the split potato slices, so that the meat is sandwiched between the potato.

Fry the mafroum: Place the flour in a shallow bowl. Dip each filled potato slice in the flour, coating lightly and shaking off the excess. In a bowl, whisk the egg, egg white, tomato paste and salt until well mixed.

Pour oil to a depth of 1.5cm (around ½ in) in a large, deep frying pan. Heat the oil over a medium heat. Dip each floured, filled potato slice in the whisked egg white mixture. Fry on both sides until golden brown, turning once. Remove using a slotted spoon and set aside.

Make the sauce: Layer a sauté pan with onion, garlic, celeriac, celery leaves and carrot. Season with salt and pepper. Pour over the tomato paste-water mixture.

Place the mafroum on top of the vegetables. Add enough water to just reach the height of the meat filling. Cover and cook over a low heat for an hour, gently shaking the pan now and then to prevent sticking, until the potatoes are tender and the sauce has thickened. Serve on its own or with couscous.

Mafroum means 'stuffed' in Moroccan. In North African Jewish cuisine there are numerous different stuffed vegetables: peppers, courgettes (zucchini), artichokes, onions.... My favourite mafroum is the one made from potatoes. They look like small, juicy meat sandwiches and are filled with flavour from the rich sauce in which they are cooked. There are many versions of this recipe but, of course, I like my mum's — nothing beats my mum's food.

CHEBBAKIA

MAKES 50 CHEBBAKIA

CHEBBAKIA DOUGH

750g (1lb 10oz) self-raising flour
180ml (¾ cup) oil
2 level tbsp coarse semolina
2 tbsp vinegar
½ tsp salt
3 drops of orange blossom essence
2 tbsp lager beer mixed with water to make up 250ml/1 cup

SUGAR SYRUP

600g (3 cups) sugar
580ml (2¼ cups) water
Juice of 1–2 lemons
Orange blossom essence

Oil for deep frying
Sesame seeds for coating

TIP: To speed up rolling out the dough, you can use a pasta machine. Lightly roll the dough, fold it and pass it through a pasta machine twice, adjusting the thickness from thicker to thinner at each stage to form 2mm (1⁄16 in) sheets.

Make the dough: Place the flour, oil, semolina, vinegar, salt and orange blossom essence in the bowl of a stand mixer. Using the K paddle, begin mixing the ingredients together, gradually adding the lager mixture to form a firm yet flexible dough. Cover the dough and set aside at room temperature to stand for 2–3 hours.

Make the sugar syrup: Half an hour before you finish resting the dough, make the sryup as you want it to be slightly warm.

Heat the sugar and water over a medium heat without stirring. Once the sugar has dissolved, add the lemon juice, reduce the heat and simmer for 5 minutes to slightly thicken the syrup. Remove from heat and flavour with orange blossom essence to taste. Set aside at room temperature.

Form the chebbakia {see photos}: Divide the rested dough into 8 balls. Take one of the balls and leave the remainder covered with a clean kitchen towel. Flatten and roll out the ball up and down on a wooden work surface to form a rough oval. Keep rolling in the same direction until the oval is around 2mm (1⁄16 in) thick. Now fold it in half and roll it once again to the same thickness. Repeat the folding and rolling process one more time.

Trim off the long edges to neaten the pastry and cut it into 8x9cm (around 3¼ x 3½ in) rectangles. Take one rectangle and cut 4 or 5 long incisions 1cm (around ¼in) apart evenly in the centre of the rectangle (making sure not to slice to the edges).

To make the traditional pastry flowers (see photos on following page), take one of the dough rectangles and thread your fingers through alternate strips so that the rest of the rectangle hangs suspended from your fingers. Turn the rectangle inside out, forming a rough flower shape. Set aside the dough flowers on a tray. Repeat the whole process with the remaining dough squares.

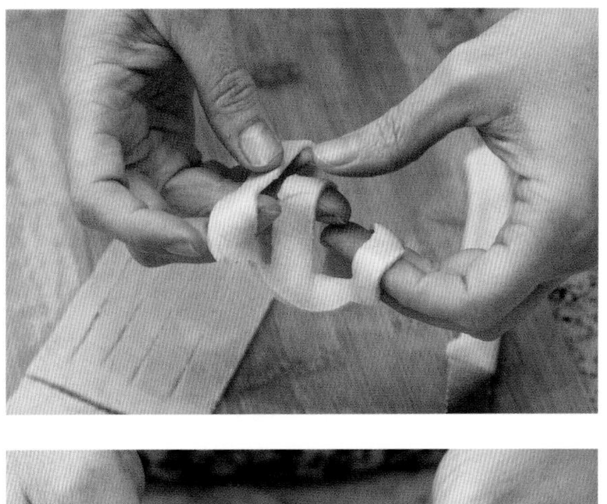

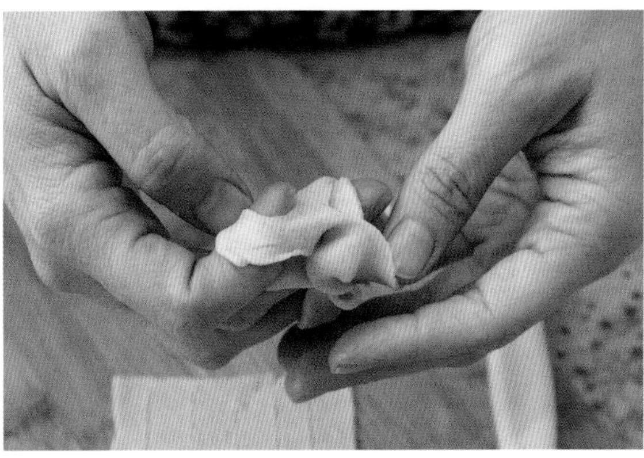

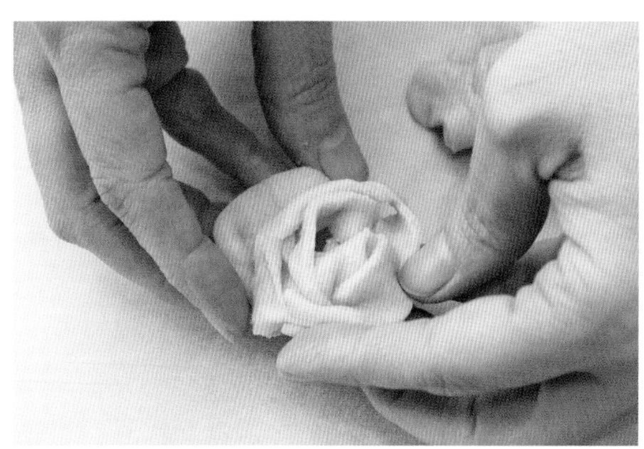

TIP: For a simpler version, rather than shaping the pastry into 'roses' just deep fry the cut rectangles.

Fry the chebbakia: Heat oil for deep frying over medium heat in a deep pot. Cook the chebbakia in batches of 4 at a time, so as not to overcrowd the pot. Gently add the chebbakia to the hot oil one at a time and fry until their colour darkens slightly, then turn carefully and fry briefly until pale gold on both sides.

Transfer the freshly fried chebbakia to a large sieve over a bowl to drain off excess oil, then use a slotted spoon to dip each warm chebbakia briefly in the sugar syrup, shaking off excess syrup. Set aside on a tray. Add a pinch of sesame seeds on top at once, so that it sticks to the warm syrup. Repeat the process with each batch. Set aside to cool and serve.

Chebbakia are a Moroccan delicacy: deep-fried pastry strips glazed with a fragrant orange-flower syrup. My late grandmother Zohara used to make these beautiful pastry roses for special occasions such as weddings or Hanukkah. Be warned: they have a particular texture and flavour which is truly addictive — once you start eating them, you can't stop!

SACHERTORTE

MAKES ONE 22CM (11IN) CAKE

CAKE

80g (3oz) dark chocolate
50g (2oz) milk chocolate
6 eggs at room temperature, separated
110g (generous ½ cup) sugar
140g (4½ oz) butter at room temperature
110g (generous ½ cup) icing (confectioners) sugar
1 tsp vanilla essence
140g (1 cup) flour, sifted

JAM GLAZE

160ml (5/8 cup) smooth apricot jam

CHOCOLATE GLAZE

200g (1 cup) sugar
125ml (½ cup) water
150g (5oz) good-quality dark chocolate

TIP: Once you've sliced the cake across into two halves, before moving the halves, insert a cocktail stick one above the other into each cake half, so that you can match the two halves up evenly when you glaze the cake.

Preheat the oven to 180°C/350°F. Butter the base and sides of a 22cm (9in) springform round cake tin, line with baking parchment and then lightly flour the whole tin.

Make the cake: Melt the dark and milk chocolate together in a bain-marie and allow to cool slightly.

Using a stand mixer, whisk the egg whites with the sugar until firm peaks form. Remove from the bowl and reserve.

In the same mixer bowl, at a medium-low speed, whisk the butter, icing sugar and vanilla essence to a smooth cream. Add the yolks one at a time, mixing well between each addition. Once all the yolks have been added, mix at a high speed for 2 minutes.

Set the stand mixer to the lowest speed and gradually add the melted chocolate to the butter mixture. Once mixed, stir in 2 tbsp of the whisked egg white to loosen the mixture, then, using a spatula, gradually fold in the remaining whisked egg white. Fold in the flour carefully but thoroughly.

Transfer the cake mix to the prepared tin. Bake for 40–50 minutes, until risen and springy. Remove from the oven, cool slightly, then carefully take out the cake and cool on a rack.

Once completely cool, freeze the cake for 20–30 minutes as this makes it easier to slice. Slice the cake across, forming two halves.

Make the jam glaze: Gently heat the jam in a small saucepan until liquid. Spread the warm jam over the bottom half of the cake. Add the top half of the cake and generously brush the glaze all over the top and sides of the cake.

Make the chocolate glaze: Heat the sugar and water in a small saucepan without stirring. Once the sugar has dissolved to form a syrup, set aside to cool slightly. Melt the dark chocolate in a bain marie. Once it has melted, add the sugar syrup, stirring until well mixed.

Place the cake on a rack on baking parchment. Pour over the warm chocolate glaze to cover the cake thoroughly and set aside at room temperature. Be patient and wait until the glaze has set before trying! Serve it with whipped cream.

TIP: This cake must be kept at room temperature, not in the fridge.

The Sachertorte looks deceptively simple, but this famous Austrian chocolate cake is a true treat. Making a good sachertorte requires concentration at every stage. When I was preparing the cake for the photoshoot, distracted by my kids in the kitchen, I didn't concentrate enough and had to make it over and over again — four times in all during one morning! I had tears in my eyes! On the fourth attempt, however, it turned out perfectly — looked great and tasted wonderful!

Neve Tzedek, Tel Aviv

PISTACHIO BAKLAVA

MAKES 24 PORTIONS

400g (14oz) pistachio kernels, chopped
1 tbsp icing sugar
250g (1 cup plus 2 tbsp) butter, melted
11 sheets of filo pastry

SUGAR SYRUP
225g (1 cup plus 2 tbsp) sugar
125ml (½ cup) water
1 tsp orange blossom water
1 tsp fresh lemon juice

Make the sugar syrup: Heat sugar and water in a saucepan over medium heat until the sugar has dissolved. Reduce the heat and simmer for 5 minutes. Stir in the orange blossom water and lemon juice. Cool and chill until required.

Mix the pistachios and icing sugar and 3 tbsp of the melted butter.

Grease a shallow-rimmed 20 x 30cm (8½ x 12in) baking tray with a little of the melted butter.

Stack the filo sheets on top of each other and slice down the middle to form two piles of rectangles and cover the filo at once to prevent it drying out.

Gently brush one of the filo rectangles with melted butter and place in the baking tray. Repeat the process with 10 more filo rectangles, forming a layer that comes slightly up the sides of the tray. Spread the pistachios in an even layer over the buttered filo.

Top with the remaining filo, brushing each rectangle with melted butter and tucking the edges down over the pistachio filling. Generously brush the final layer with melted butter. Cover and chill in the refrigerator for 15–20 minutes, in order to firm it up.

Preheat the oven to 180°C/350°F.

With a sharp knife, cut the baklava right through all the layers into 24 squares. Bake for 45 minutes until crisp and golden.

Remove the baklava from the oven and rest for 2 minutes. Using a tablespoon, gently spoon the cold syrup over the hot baklava. Set it aside to cool to room temperature and absorb the syrup.

The baklava will keep at room temperature for 2 days, then refrigerate it after that.

I love to walk around the markets in Tel Aviv and Jaffa. Among the sights I enjoy are the stalls piled high with magnificent displays of baklava — tempting golden-brown, syrup-laden pastries in assorted shapes, filled with different nuts such as walnuts or almonds, cream cheese or custard. Pistachio baklava, which are the most expensive, are my favourite, as I think they have the best flavour. Try this recipe for yourself and you will see what I mean.

ROSETTA – ALMOND SYRUP

MAKES AROUND 1.5 LITRES (6 CUPS)

250g (9oz) raw almonds, skin on
1.25 ltr (5 cups) water
900g (4½ cups) sugar
½ tsp good-quality almond essence

Place the almonds in a bowl and cover with boiling water. Drain and use your fingers to squeeze the almonds from their skins.

Make almond milk: Finely grind the skinned almonds in a food processor with 250ml (1 cup) cold water for around 2 minutes. Stop the food processor now and then and scrape down the sides. Process until the mixture forms a thick paste.

Place the almond paste in the middle of a piece of muslin cheesecloth, wrap the muslin up around the paste and squeeze out the almond milk into a large, deep saucepan.

Return the squeezed almond paste to the food processor. Add 250ml (1 cup) water and process again for 1 minute to mix well. Squeeze out the liquid through the muslin once again, adding it to the almond milk in the saucepan. Repeat this process a third time.

Make a sugar syrup: Place the sugar and 500ml (2 cups) water in a large saucepan. Cook over a medium heat until the sugar has dissolved, then bring to the boil, reduce the heat, and simmer uncovered for 10 minutes, until thickened into a syrup.

Make the almond syrup: Add the almond milk to the syrup. Stir and cook for 1 minute. Stir in the almond essence; taste and add more almond essence if required. Cool, transfer to a bottle and refrigerate. Shake well before using.

Make the rosetta: Dilute the almond syrup to taste with cold water, add ice and serve.

In the 1970s in Tel Aviv any new food or drink that appeared was very exciting. My dad would always buy new drinks for us to try. By the age of ten I had tasted piña colada, Irish cream and mint liqueur! Then in Jaffa he discovered a delicious new drink — Rosetta, an almond syrup, which I loved. When I moved to London I couldn't find a kosher Rosetta, so my dad tracked down the recipe for me from the original Jaffa maker. Now I make it myself and drinking it reminds me of home. On a hot summer's day, a thirst-quenching glass of Rosetta with lots of ice is to me the perfect drink.

Tea Time

COMING TO LONDON

I was fascinated by England and its Royal family when I was a little girl. My father used to tell me fond stories about the British. As a boy, he liked British manners, the British accent and of course, British pop music, especially the Beatles. He has kept the British shilling coins from his childhood to this day. I was disappointed that the British had left Israel because I wanted to be part of the Empire. I felt a fond connection to England when I watched David Copperfield and The Secret Garden on TV or read the books.

I hoped that one day I'd come to England to see the rolling green countryside with it's majestic castles and one of the greatest cities in the world — London. Be careful what you wish for! About 20 years later my dear husband brought me to live in London, to Stamford Hill to be precise. It was tough when I got here. I came from sunny Tel Aviv, with its white houses and the Mediterranean Sea with its soft sandy beaches, to London's suburbs with their dark brown brick houses and — all too often — gloomy, rainy weather! I left my loving family and friends for an unfamiliar Jewish community: The Hassidim.

I have come to appreciate the warmth of the Stamford Hill community. The people are humble, friendly and live modestly. They are always willing to help anyone in need. Charitable giving is vital and there is a duty of care to help those less fortunate. There are special organisations and charities that work to feed the hungry, provide a free 24-hour first aid service or visit sick people in hospitals, keeping them company and bringing them kosher food. Besides, Stamford Hill is the only place in the world where you can find Yemenite Jews who speak Yiddish fluently! Another advantage is the variety of kosher food shops, including the best kosher butchers and fishmongers (fish sellers), willing to prepare your meat and fish in any way you like: cut or minced, skin on or off, bones in or out, and deliver it to your home.

The biggest surprise has been the harmony that exists in this part of London where people of different faiths all live peacefully side by side. There are synagogues, mosques and churches in the neighbourhood. They all work together especially when it comes to food. In the local kosher butchers, fishmongers, grocers and household stores, there are Muslims, Christians and Hindus working alongside Jews. My recipe for Hamsi was kindly given to me by a Turkish Muslim fishmonger called Volkan, who came to my house to help prepare it. There is a lot of mutual respect.

Springfield Park, Stamford Hill, London

CRAFTED
53

David & Yoeli in Primrose Hill

JAM SANDWICH COOKIES

MAKES AROUND 25 SANDWICH COOKIES

200g (⅞ cup) butter, softened
100g (1 cup) icing (confectioners) sugar
1 tsp vanilla essence
300g (2 cups plus 2 tbsp) flour, sifted
4 tbsp milk
¼ tsp salt

Icing (confectioners) sugar, to decorate
Smooth strawberry jam, for filling

TIP: If you want your cookies to be extra crisp and stay fresh for longer, see Limi's Notes and Tips p.392.

Place the butter, icing sugar and vanilla essence in the bowl of a stand mixer. Using the K-paddle, mix at a medium-low speed until combined.

Add half the flour, the milk and the salt and mix until smooth. Add the remaining flour and mix to form a soft dough. Wrap in film and chill for 2 hours.

Preheat the oven to 180°C/350°F. Line 2 baking trays with baking parchment.

Working on a floured surface, roll the dough finely to a thickness of 2mm (around ⅒ in).

Using a circular or flower-shaped cutter (approx. 5cm/2in across), cut out 50 cookie shapes. Next, use a smaller circular or flower-shaped cutter (approx. 2cm/0.8in) to cut out holes in the centre of 25 of the cookie shapes.

Place the whole cookie shapes, spaced well apart, on one baking tray. Place the ones with holes cut out on the other baking tray. Bake the cookies for 12 minutes until pale golden. Remove and cool completely.

Sift icing (confectioners) sugar over the cookies with holes.

Place ½ tsp of strawberry jam in the centre of each of the whole cookies. Gently top the jam-topped cookies with the sugar-coated cookies, pressing them together gently.

These are everyone's childhood cookies. They used to be sold in shops loose by weight or in biscuit tins. Two butter cookies and a jam filling — every child's perfect sandwich!

GURAIBE

MAKES AROUND 50

50 roasted salted pistachio kernels
150g (5oz) butter, softened
120g (4oz) soft margarine
4 tbsp oil
¼ tsp baking powder
1 tsp vanilla essence
1–2 tbsp Maz-har (orange blossom water)
400g (3 cups) flour
¾ cup icing sugar
1 heaped tbsp caster (superfine) sugar

Blanch the pistachio kernels in a bowl of boiling water for 3–5 minutes. Drain and gently rub and pick off the papery skins, taking care to keep them whole. Pat dry with kitchen paper and set aside.

Place all the ingredients apart from the pistachios in the bowl of a stand mixer. Using the K-paddle, mix them together to form a soft dough.

Preheat the oven to 150°C/300°F. Line 2 baking trays with baking parchment.

Shape the dough into small ping pong-sized balls. Place these, spaced well apart, on the baking trays. Slightly flatten each dough ball and gently press a pistachio kernel into the centre of each one.

Bake for 35 minutes until light golden in colour. Remove and cool before serving.

Guraibe are biscuits from Syria and Lebanon that have a special place in our family. Every time my father comes to visit me in London he begs that I will make Guraibe for him. 'No way!' I say, 'You're not meant to eat sweet, buttery biscuits!' Then, when he arrives at our house, I surprise him by serving Guraibe. I love seeing his face light up when he sets his eyes on them!

TAHINI COOKIES

MAKES APPROX. 40

200g (7/8 cup) butter, softened
100g (1/2 cup) caster (superfine) sugar
70g (1/2 cup) icing (confectioners) sugar
1 tsp vanilla essence
Pinch of salt
320g (1 1/4 cup) tahini
420g (3 level cups) flour

FOR DECORATION

Walnut halves or whole blanched almonds

TIP: If you want your cookies to be extra crisp and stay fresh for longer, see Limi's Notes and Tips p.392.

Using a stand mixer with the K-paddle, mix together the butter, both types of sugar and vanilla essence at a medium speed until well mixed, scraping down the sides as you go. Add salt and tahini, and mix together well. Add in the flour and mix in at a slow speed, working in short bursts, being careful not to over mix and scraping down between mixing. As soon as the mixture comes together to form a soft, sticky dough, it is ready. Wrap in film and chill for 1 hour.

Preheat oven to 160°C/325°F. Line two baking trays with baking parchment.

Shape the dough into walnut-sized balls. Place the balls, spaced well apart, on the lined baking trays. Press each ball down gently to form a round shape. Gently press a nut on top of each cookie.

Bake for 25–30 minutes until pale gold. Allow the cookies to cool and set before eating.

Kikar Atarim, Tel Aviv

You always feel less guilty when you eat cookies made from a healthy ingredient! These melt-in-your-mouth Middle Eastern cookies go wonderfully with a cup of strong Turkish coffee.

PURIM HAMANTASHCEN

MAKES AROUND 45

FOR THE DOUGH
125g (½ cup) cold butter, cubed
75g (⅓ cup) cold margarine, cubed
½ tsp baking powder
350g (2½ cups) flour
65g (⅓ cup) sugar
65g (⅓ cup) icing (confectioners) sugar
Pinch of salt
1 tsp vanilla essence
2 egg yolks
Grated zest of ½ lemon
4 tbsp brandy or whisky

FOR THE FILLING
250ml (1 cup) of jam or chocolate spread

FOR DECORATING
Icing (confectioners) sugar

In a stand mixer with a K-paddle, make the dough by briefly mixing together the butter, margarine, baking powder, flour, both sugars, salt and vanilla essence until the mixture resembles crumbs.

Add yolks, lemon zest and brandy and mix briefly until it comes together. If the mixture doesn't come together, add 1–2 tbsp water or milk as needed. Take care not to over-mix. Wrap the pastry in film and chill in the fridge for an hour.

Preheat the oven to 180°C/350°F.Line 2 baking trays with baking parchment.

Roll out the pastry on a sheet of floured baking parchment to a 3–4mm (around ¼ in) thickness. Using a circular 7cm (3in) cutter, cut out discs from the pastry. Gather together the pastry trimmings, work together and roll out to make more discs.

To make each hamantasch, place ½ a teaspoon of the filling in the centre of each pastry disc. Bring three sides of the pastry partly up over the filling, leaving it exposed in the centre, and pinch the corners to form a neat, triangular shape. Repeat the process until all the discs have been used.

Place the hamantaschen on trays and chill them in the fridge for 15 minutes. Transfer to the lined baking trays and bake for 20 minutes until lightly golden. Cool completely, dust with icing (confectioners) sugar and serve. Store in an airtight container.

These sweet pastries are made and eaten during the Jewish festival of Purim. Their Hebrew name means 'Haman's ears' and their distinctive triangular shape symbolises the ears of Haman, the historic Persian vizier who wanted to kill all the Jews in the Persian empire. Haman's plans were foiled and the festival of Purim celebrates the saving of the Jewish people with 'Haman's ears' eaten to mark his downfall. The traditional filling is made from poppy seeds, but jam or chocolate spread have become very popular.

Celebrating Purim,
Limi (middle) with her cousins

STEEL
WORKS
LN02 TZC

SALTY-SWEET BUTTER HERB BISCUITS

MAKES AROUND 45 BISCUITS

225g butter (1 cup), softened
3 tbsp olive oil
1 tsp fine salt
½ tsp coarse sea salt (I like to use Maldon)
4½ tbsp icing (confectioners) sugar
2 tbsp sugar
250g (1¾ cups) flour, sifted
50g (4 tbsp) cornflour (corn starch)
1 tbsp mixed herbs (such as finely chopped fresh rosemary and thyme leaves or ½ tsp oregano and 2½ tsp za'atar)

TOPPING

Water, for brushing
Coarse sea salt
Za'atar

TIP: If you want your cookies to be extra crisp and stay fresh for longer, see Limi's Notes and Tips p.392.

Using a stand mixer with a K blade, mix together the butter and olive oil at medium speed for 2–3 minutes, scraping the sides as you do so.

Add in the fine and coarse salt, icing sugar and sugar and mix briefly. Add in the flour, cornflour (corn starch) and herbs. Mix until the ingredients come together to form a soft dough. Wrap and chill for 3 hours.

Preheat the oven to 180°C/350°F.

Place half of the chilled dough on a floured sheet of baking parchment and flatten to 5mm (around ¼ in) thickness. Using a knife, cut the dough into 7 x 3cm (2½ in x 1¼ in) rectangles. At this stage the dough is very soft, so transfer the rectangles, still on the baking parchment on a tray, to the freezer for 15 minutes. Repeat the process with the remaining dough.

Line two large baking trays with parchment. Transfer the chilled biscuits to these large lined baking trays, making sure to space them well apart. Lightly brush each biscuit with water and sprinkle over coarse sea salt and za'atar.

Bake the biscuits (in batches if need be) for around 15 minutes, until the edges are golden. Cool and store in airtight containers, where they will keep for at least a week.

"Whenever I make these biscuits, my guests are always intrigued — the results are buttery with a delicate salty-sweet flavour which plays with your tastebuds when you eat them!"

CHOCOLATE PUFF FINGERS

MAKES AROUND 20

800g (1lb 12oz) puff pastry sheets, 16 x 20cm (around 6 x 8in) in size
40 dark chocolate sticks or 20 rows of good quality cooking dark/milk chocolate squares from bars, each row sliced in half lengthways

GLAZE
1 beaten egg
40g (4 tbsp) butter, melted and cooled

Demerara (soft brown) sugar, for topping

TIP: I like to mix milk and dark chocolate, to get both sweetness and a good chocolate flavour.

Preheat the oven to 180°C/350°F. Line 2 baking trays with baking paper.

Cut each puff pastry sheet into 6 squares approximately 8 x 10cm (3 x 4in). You want the pastry to be slightly less wide than the chocolate sticks.

Take a pastry square, place one stick near the edge, roll it over once, then put a second stick in alongside it. Roll the pastry over to cover both chocolate sticks and trim off any excess pastry. Pinch the pastry together to seal. Repeat.

Mix the glaze ingredients together. Take each pastry finger and dip its surface in the glaze. Place on a lined baking tray and sprinkle with sugar.

Bake the chocolate fingers for 25 minutes until golden. Serve warm or at room temperature.

This quick and easy recipe is perfect for when you don't have time to make pain au chocolat but want to give your family a treat — and you can spend quality time with your children by making them together!

STAR

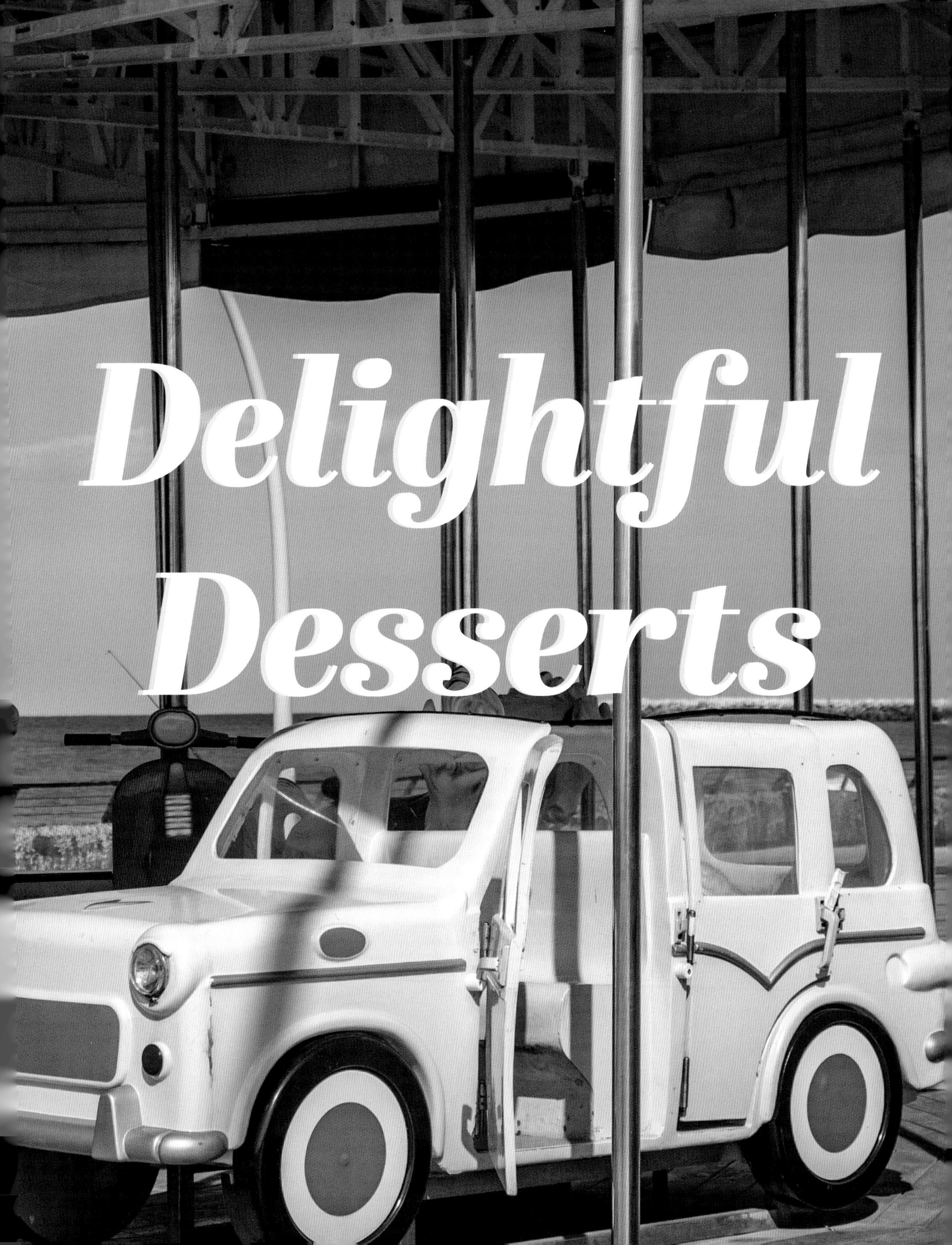

Delightful Desserts

MALABI

SERVES 10–12

FOR THE MALABI
2 litres (8 cups) milk or water
6 tbsp sugar
140g (1⅛ cup) cornflour (corn starch)
A few drops of orange blossom water

FOR THE TOPPING
Grenadine syrup or raspberry syrup
Desiccated coconut
Roasted pistachio kernels or peanuts, chopped

TIP: For a richer flavour and creamier texture if using water to make the malabi, substitute 250ml (1 cup) canned coconut milk for 250ml (1 cup) of the water.

Cook the malabi: In a large saucepan, over a medium heat, heat 1.6 litres (around 6 cups) of the milk or water and the sugar, stirring now and then until the sugar has dissolved.

Mix together the remaining liquid with the cornflour (corn starch), stirring thoroughly until no lumps remain.

Bring the liquid to boiling point. Using a whisk, mix it constantly and gradually add the cornflour (corn starch) mixture until it becomes thoroughly absorbed. Mix for a further minute to ensure a smooth texture. Remove from direct heat. Add the orange blossom water and mix in.

Cool and set the malabi: Pour it into a large metal serving dish, cool thoroughly, then cover and chill for 2 days until set. Alternately, for individual portions, divide the mixture evenly among 10–12 small, shallow serving bowls, cool thoroughly, cover and chill overnight to set.

To serve the large malabi, invert it onto a serving plate, knock on the top of the dish once or twice to release the malabi, and lift the dish off. Top with grenadine syrup, desiccated coconut and pistachios. To serve the small malabi, simply garnish each portion in its bowl as above.

Malabi can be kept in the fridge for up to 3 days.

Traditionally, malabi was made using water. Over time, people began using milk instead. Always served cold, it is a much-loved, refreshing street food dessert, enjoyed in countries such as Turkey and Syria. In recent decades, chefs have started making fancier versions to serve in their restaurants. They use cream rather than water to make it richer, which I'm not convinced is an improvement. Using water or milk gives the malabi its jelly-like texture, which is part of the pleasure of eating it. Some people flavour it with rose water, but I prefer orange blossom water.

I have happy memories of eating malabi in my childhood, as on the weekend my dad would take us to eat it either in Tel Aviv or Jaffa. We would visit humble little places that specialised only in malabi and sit there enjoying the cool dessert and the variety of toppings.

70s COMPOTE

SERVES 4

500ml (2 cups) freshly squeezed orange juice
Sugar to taste
3–4 ripe bananas
15 strawberries
Mint leaves, to decorate

Place the orange juice in a serving bowl. Sweeten with sugar to taste, stirring it in until thoroughly dissolved.

Slice the bananas and the strawberries and add to the orange juice, mixing well to coat. Cover and chill for an hour before serving.

Serve in small bowls, decorated with a few mint leaves.

In Israel every household has its own version of a fruit compote. Some use dried fruit, others cooked fruit, but in the 1970s in Tel Aviv this recipe was very popular and is the one my mother used to make. It's very simple, but on a hot summer's day it is so refreshing — like eating and drinking at once. Sweet and delicious — and healthy too!

KADAIF

MAKES 10 PORTIONS

450g (1lb) kadaif pastry (thoroughly defrosted if frozen)
200g (⅞ cup) unsalted butter, melted
500ml (2 cups) whipping cream
2 tbsp icing (confectioners) sugar
3–4 tbsp sugar

SUGAR SYRUP
300g (1½ cups) sugar
250ml (1 cup) water
1 tbsp lemon juice
1–2 tsp orange blossom water

FOR DECORATION
Roasted pistachio kernels, chopped

Make the sugar syrup: Heat the sugar and water in a small saucepan until dissolved, bring nearly to the boil and simmer for 3–4 minutes. Remove from direct heat and stir in the lemon juice and orange blossom water. Set aside.

Prepare the pastry: Preheat the oven to 180°C/350°F. Line a baking tray with baking parchment.

Place the kadaif pastry in a bowl. Pour over the melted butter and use your hands to rub it thoroughly with the pastry, coating all the strands, and tearing slightly to shorten them. Spread the kadaif in a fine, even layer on the baking tray, pulling it apart to separate any clumps as you do so.

Bake it in the oven for around 20–30 minutes, until golden. Remove from the oven and, using a spoon, drizzle over enough syrup to moisten it slightly. Set aside to cool completely.

Assemble the kadaif: Using a circular pastry cutter or a sharp knife, cut out 10 discs from the cooled kadaif and use these to snugly line 10 small containers or serving bowls. Crumble the remaining kadaif to use for the topping and set aside.

Make the filling by whisking together the cream, icing (confectioners) sugar and 3 tbsp of sugar until fluffy. Taste and add 1 tbsp more sugar if needed.

Top each kadaif base with a 2cm (¾ in) layer of the cream. Sprinkle over a thin layer of the crumbled kadaif. Cover and chill for 3–4 hours to set. Sprinkle over the pistachios just before serving.

Kadaif is the name of both the shredded pastry and the confections made from it. This combination of crisp, sweet, golden kadaif and soft, fluffy cream is blissful!

At weekends, when my father took me with him to visit Jaffa, we would come across large Arabic shops filled with sweet treats. I vividly remember looking between the different baklava and spotting stacks of cream-topped kadaif desserts — each portion in its own little round see-through container — which I found so tempting, that inevitably my father would succumb and buy me at least one!

'Flowers for Shabbat'

מיני
מנוי

APPLE PIE

MAKES ONE 20CM (8IN) PIE

FILLING

30g (2 tbsp) butter

1.2kg (2½ lb) Granny Smith apples, peeled, cored, chopped into chunks

Juice of ½ lemon

80g (6 tbsp) sugar

½ tsp vanilla essence

Pinch of ground cinnamon (optional)

1 tbsp dry breadcrumbs

PASTRY

250g (9oz) flour

125g (½ cup) butter

125g (⅔ cup) sugar

1 tsp lemon juice

1 egg

Icing sugar, for dusting

Whipped cream, for serving

Make the filling: Melt the butter in a frying pan over medium heat. Add the apple chunks, mix in the lemon juice and cook, stirring often, for 5 minutes. Add the sugar, vanilla essence and cinnamon and cook, stirring often, for 5–8 minutes more, until the apple is partly softened and most of the excess moisture has been cooked off. Set aside to cool thoroughly.

Make the pastry: Preheat the oven to 180°C/350°F. Grease a 20cm (8in) springform round cake tin.

Place the flour, butter, sugar, lemon juice and egg in the bowl of a stand mixer. Using the K-paddle, mix until the ingredients come together and form a pastry ball.

Take a third of the pastry (wrapping and chilling the remainder), and press it into the base of the cake tin to make a thin layer of pastry. Prick the pastry case all over with a fork and bake for 10 minutes, then remove from the oven.

Sprinkle the breadcrumbs evenly over the pastry base. Top with the cooled, cooked apple, spreading it out in an even layer.

Roll out the remaining pastry on a lightly floured surface to a thickness of 5mm (around ¼ in) and cut it into 1.5cm (around ½ in) thick strips. Arrange the pastry strips over the apple slices in a lattice pattern, weaving the strips over and under if desired.

Bake the apple pie for 45 minutes, until nicely golden. Sprinkle with icing sugar and serve warm with whipped cream.

My husband is very fond of apples, so I have at least seven recipes for cakes and desserts that use apples. This apple pie is one I make for special occasions, as it's rich and delicious. I like to cook the apple first as this removes the excess moisture, which would otherwise make the pie base soggy.

70s SAVARIN CAKE

MAKES ONE 20CM (8IN) CAKE

FOR THE CAKE
105g (4/5 cup) self-raising flour
3 tbsp dry breadcrumbs
½ tsp baking powder
100g (½ cup) sugar
227g (8oz) tub of sour cream
2 eggs

250ml (1 cup) cold water

SUGAR SYRUP
200g (1 cup) sugar
250ml (1 cup) water
1 tsp vanilla essence
1 tbsp rum

TOPPING
3–4 tbsp strawberry or apricot jam
250ml (1 cup) whipping cream
2 tbsp sugar
½ tbsp Vanilla Instant Pudding
8 Amarena cherries in syrup, for decoration

Preheat the oven to 170°C/340°F. Grease a 20cm (8in) springform round cake tin.

In a mixing bowl, vigorously mix all the cake ingredients (apart from the water) together to form a smooth batter. Transfer to the cake tin and level. Bake for 40 minutes until golden-brown on top. Test by inserting a skewer into the centre of the cake; if it comes out clean and dry, the cake is ready.

Remove the cake from the oven. Pour 250ml (1 cup) of cold water evenly over the cake, soaking it well. Set aside to cool completely.

Make the sugar syrup: Heat the sugar and water in a small saucepan until dissolved, bring nearly to the boil, and simmer for 3–4 minutes. Remove from heat and stir in the vanilla essence and the rum.

Wait 5 minutes to allow the syrup to cool slightly, then spoon the warm syrup evenly all over the cake. Set aside to cool completely.

Make the topping: Gently heat the jam in a small saucepan, stirring, until liquid. Spread the jam in an even layer over the top of the cake and allow to cool.

Whisk the cream, sugar and Instant Pudding together until fluffy. Pipe this over the cake, decorate with the cherries, and serve.

A big hit in Israel in the 1960s and 1970s, the savarin comes originally from France. When I was a child, I remember seeing it in all the cafés in Tel Aviv. The best one came from a small café in King George Street. As a little girl with my mother, I would stop to gaze at the mouth-watering display in the window. For a treat now and then we would go into the café and share just one individual savarin, as they were so rich, moist and delicious! This recipe is for a yeast-free version and very easy to make at home.

Dan Hotel, Tel Aviv

SNOW ICE CREAM

SERVES 12–14

- 750ml (3 cups) whipping cream
- 100g (3½ oz) meringue, powdered
- 1 tsp vanilla essence (optional)
- 3 heaped tbsp strawberry sorbet (see recipe p.322)
- ice cream wafers, to serve

Place the cream, powdered meringue and vanilla essence (if using) in the bowl of a stand mixer. Using the whisk attachment, whisk until light and fluffy.

Transfer half the mixture to a freezer-proof container (24cm (9½ in) square) spreading it in an even layer.

In a small bowl, stir the strawberry sorbet until just melted. Add to the remaining cream mixture and whisk in briefly, tinting it pale pink. Spread this lightly and evenly over the first layer. Cover and freeze until set.

To serve, cut the ice cream in slices to fit your ice cream wafers, making sure to get both the white and pink ice cream. Place an ice cream slice between two wafers and enjoy!

TIP: As an option to the strawberry sorbet, use 150g (5oz) chopped strawberries, blended with 3–4 tbsp icing sugar instead.

In Tel Aviv during the 70s there was a small shop close to the beach called Snow Ice Cream, which my dad would take us to for a weekend treat. They sold ice cream, made from sweetened whipped cream, served between crisp wafers, which we call 'cassata' in Israel. As simple as it sounds, the taste of this pink and white ice cream slice was heavenly. Sadly, this legendary place closed many years ago; to this day, the people of Tel Aviv still remember it fondly. I always wanted to taste Snow Ice Cream again and this recipe is the closest I can come to it.

GELA
מותק של גלידה

סיפון
דרומי
חוף מציצים
Metzitzim
Beach

SHARON

SORBETS

When I make sorbet, I don't use egg whites as many people do — as I have a dislike for raw eggs. I find store-bought sorbets far too sweet for my taste. My sorbets are made using just natural ingredients and sugar syrup and without a special ice cream maker. Making your own allows you to create wonderful sorbets in which the natural flavours of the ingredients come to the fore.

When making sorbets, you need to use a sugar syrup as its low freezing point helps create a good creamy texture. Using fruits that have a lot of body and fibre — mangoes, bananas, apricots, berries — gives a lovely texture to sorbets, making them less icy and more like ice cream. Apart from bananas, when using a fruit purée as the sorbet base, I usually blend it to remove any fibres, as this gives a smoother texture. If I'm making a sorbet using ingredients that have less body — like lemon juice — then I always add 1–2 tbsp of vodka, a pinch of salt and more sugar syrup in order to get the soft texture I'm looking for. The great thing about having a good basic sorbet recipe is that you can then experiment with different flavour combinations and be creative — I love trying out new variations!

SORBET TIP: For a quickly-made ice cream with a creamier texture, substitute frozen fruit for fresh fruit in the recipe and mix it only once or twice, rather than three times.

SUGAR SYRUP FOR SORBETS

300g (1½ cups) sugar
100ml (5 fl oz) water
Freshly squeezed juice of ½ lemon

Gently heat the sugar and water in a small saucepan, without stirring, until the sugar has dissolved. Simmer for 3–4 minutes, remove from direct heat, stir in the lemon juice and set aside to cool.

BANANA CHOCOLATE CHIP SORBET

MAKES AROUND 1.5–2 LITRES (6–8 CUPS)

8 large, ripe bananas
Freshly squeezed juice of ½ lemon
A pinch of ground cinnamon (optional)
1 quantity of cooled sugar syrup (see p.316)
150g (5oz) dark chocolate chips

In a large jug blender, blend together the bananas, lemon juice and cinnamon (if using) into a smooth purée.

Add the sugar syrup and blitz again until thoroughly blended. Now taste the mixture and check for sweetness. Bear in mind that when frozen it will taste slightly less sweet. If you feel it needs to be sweeter, add 1–2 tbsp of icing sugar and blend in well.

Transfer the mixture to a lidded, freezer-proof container and freeze overnight or for at least 6 hours until frozen and set.

Transfer the sorbet mixture to a stand mixer bowl. Using the K-paddle, mix it, breaking it down, until it resembles a thick cream. Add the chocolate chips and mix in briefly. Return the mixture to the container and freeze overnight or for at least 6 hours.

Mix the frozen sorbet once more in the stand mixer bowl until creamy. Place in the freezer-proof container and store in the freezer until needed.

"My family love my home-made sorbets and prefer them to the store-bought ones. Banana and chocolate is a classic flavour combination and this is one of my boys' favourites."

The First Hebrew Carousel, port of Tel Aviv

PINEAPPLE MINT SORBET

MAKES AROUND 500ML (2 CUPS)

- 2 ripe medium pineapples, peeled, trimmed, cored and chopped into small chunks
- Juice of ½ lemon
- 1 quantity of sugar syrup (see p.316)
- A handful of mint leaves, chopped

In a large jug blender, thoroughly blend the pineapple and lemon juice till smooth. Pass the mixture through a sieve.

Return the pineapple purée to the blender, add the sugar syrup and blend to mix well. Now taste the mixture and check for sweetness. Bear in mind that when frozen it will taste slightly less sweet. If you feel it needs to be sweeter, add 1–2 tbsp of icing sugar and blend in well. Add the mint and blend briefly just until the mint is finely chopped; take care not to over-mix or you will have a green sorbet!

Place mixture in a lidded, freezer-proof container and freeze overnight or for at least 6 hours until set. Transfer to a stand mixer bowl; using the K-paddle, mix until creamy. Return to the container; freeze overnight or for at least 6 hours.

Mix the frozen sorbet once more in the stand mixer bowl until creamy. Store in the freezer.

STRAWBERRY SORBET

MAKES AROUND 1.5–2 LITRES (6–8 CUPS)

- 1kg (2lb 4oz) strawberries, hulled and roughly chopped
- Juice of ½ lemon
- 1 tsp vanilla essence
- 1 quantity of cooled sugar syrup (see p.316)

In a large jug blender, blend the strawberries, lemon juice and vanilla essence till smooth. Pass the mixture through a sieve.

Return the strawberry purée to the blender, add the sugar syrup and blend to mix well. Now taste the mixture and check for sweetness. Bear in mind that when frozen it will taste slightly less sweet. If you feel it needs to be sweeter, add 1–2 tbsp of icing sugar and blend in well.

Place mixture in a lidded, freezer-proof container and freeze overnight or for at least 6 hours until set. Transfer to a stand mixer bowl; using the K-paddle, mix until creamy. Return to the container; freeze overnight or for at least 6 hours.

Mix the frozen sorbet once more in the stand mixer bowl until creamy. Store in the freezer.

EAT MORE FRUIT AND KEEP FIT
STX
גרוב אדום
מנגנון הנפש
גרוב אדום
תודה ולהתראות

Drinks

LEMONADE

SERVES 5–6

FOR THE LEMONADE SYRUP

200g (1 cup) sugar

250ml (1 cup) water

Grated zest of 1 lemon (optional)

250ml freshly squeezed lemon juice, strained

1–1.25 litres (4–5 cups) cold water

TO SERVE

Ice cubes

Mint leaves

Lemon slices

Place all the syrup ingredients in a small saucepan and bring to the boil; simmer until slightly thickened, around 2–3 minutes. Strain, mix in the lemon juice, stirring well, and set aside to cool.

To make the lemonade, dilute the syrup with cold water, mixing well. Serve it with ice cubes, mint leaves and lemon slices.

On a hot summer's day, there is a special pleasure to drinking a cold glass of fresh lemonade. As a child in Tel Aviv, walking through Carmel Market, on my way back from school, I would always stop at the lemonade stall — with its huge container of lemonade and ice — and buy myself a glass of icy cold lemonade with my pocket money. Such a treat!

PALOODA

SERVES 10

200g (7oz) rice vermicelli
Amarena cherries and syrup, to serve

SYRUP
600g (3 cups) sugar
2.25 litres (around 9 cups) water
Juice of 1 lemon
3 drops rose extract or 1 tbsp rose water

Make the syrup: Dissolve the sugar with the water in a saucepan over medium heat without stirring. Once the sugar has dissolved, stir in the lemon juice and taste the syrup to check its sweetness. If too sweet for your taste, add a further 250ml of water and bring to the boil, then turn off the heat. If not sweet enough, add 1 tbsp sugar to the simmering syrup, allow it to dissolve and taste again. Turn off the heat, stir in the rose flavouring and set aside to cool.

Soak the rice vermicelli in boiling water until just softened (it's important they retain their texture). Drain and rinse them thoroughly in cold water.

Place the softened noodles in the cool syrup and stir to mix them in. Transfer to a freezer-proof container. Freeze the noodle mixture for 6–8 hours until it is half frozen and stir again to spread the noodles through the mixture evenly. Return to the freezer.

The night before you want to serve it, transfer to the fridge so that it softens to a slush.

Serve in tall glasses, each topped with an amarena cherry and a tbsp of the cherry syrup poured over the top.

I first came across this drink when I was living and working in Tel Aviv. It was a very hot day and my car's air conditioning had stopped working. Then, as I drove along, I saw in the middle of the road a small stall with a sign saying 'Palooda — a Persian rosewater drink'. The seller had a large container of a whitish liquid with noodles floating inside. I pulled over and bought a cup. With ice and noodles it was the most beautiful and unusual drink I'd ever seen, and so refreshing and delicious that I had to buy a second cupful! Ever since then, I'd often wondered how to make it and when a kind Persian friend of mine gave me the recipe, I was thrilled. The amarena cherry is my own touch — it looks so dramatic against the white drink and tastes wonderful too.

FRESH MINT TEA

SERVES 4

4 generous handfuls of fresh mint
8 tsp sugar (or to taste)
1 Assam or English Breakfast teabag

Take four heatproof glass cups. Place a handful of the mint and 2 tsp sugar in each cup. Pour in boiling water to scald the leaves, stir and leave for 30 seconds. Take the teabag and dip it briefly into each cup to add a touch of colour. Stir once more.

Pour the tea, including the leaves, into a teapot. Holding the teapot high, pour the tea back into the hot cups, creating a slight foam on the surface, The more bubbles the better the tea. Serve at once, preferably with Guraibe (see p.283) or Tahini Cookies (see p.284).

Mint tea always reminds me of my beloved, late Grandmother Zohara. She had a large garden filled with herbs and growing among them was the best mint in the world. Every morning she would pick a small bunch and put it in a glass of water on the work surface in her kitchen. Whenever I visited, she would make me at least 3 cups of mint tea. In Morocco, we always drink our mint tea sweet and from glass cups. I remember how she poured the tea from her metal teapot from very high into the cups — 'the more air the better,' she said. Hot, sweet mint tea is to me a heart-warming drink.

HOT CHOCOLATE

SERVES 4

1 litre (4 cups) full-fat milk
4 heaped tsp cocoa powder
8–9 tsp sugar (or to taste)

Place all the ingredients in a saucepan. Heat over a medium heat, whisking constantly, to blend thoroughly. As soon as it reaches boiling point, remove from direct heat and pour into 4 mugs. Serve at once.

In the 1970s mothers gave us spinach to make us strong like Popeye, milk to give us white teeth — and chocolate so that we would leave them in peace. My mother must have really wanted us to have white teeth and to be left in peace, as she made us hot chocolate every day from the age of 4–17! This is proper home-made hot chocolate, not made using a shop-bought mixture. I make hot chocolate for my sons almost every day and sometimes, before I serve it, absent mindedly drink half myself out of habit.

Café Danon c 1940,
Mahaneh Yehuda market

TURKISH COFFEE

SERVES 2

2 heaped tsp of very finely ground Turkish coffee (see tip)
Sugar, to taste
350ml (1½ cup) water

TIP: Alternatively, add 2–3 cardamom pods or ¼ tsp ground cardamom to the coffee mixture in the pot. This gives a lovely fragrance and flavour to the coffee.

Place the coffee, sugar and water in a cezve (Turkish coffee pot) or a small saucepan. Heat over a medium heat, stirring constantly, until it comes just to boiling point. The instant you see the foam, pour it into small coffee cups. Pour carefully to distribute the foam between each serving.

Serve the coffee with a glass of cold water and Guraibe (see p.283) or Tahini Cookies (see p.284) on the side.

Tel Aviv is fuelled by the drinking of Turkish coffee, a small, powerful drink that is a great way to wake up. Israelis love it so much that they've even written a song about it! The phrase 'Turkish coffee' refers to the extremely fine grind of the coffee used to make it. This is the way coffee was historically made in the Ottoman Empire. The finer the grind, the fewer the floating coffee grounds in the cup. Ideally, when it's served, there should be a little central gap in the foam in the cup — this is the most elegant way to present it. Once the coffee has been drunk, it is a tradition to turn the cup over and tell one's fortune from the shapes formed by the coffee grounds.

FRUIT SMOOTHIES

MAKES 1–2 SERVINGS, DEPENDING ON GLASS SIZE

The ratio I use is 250ml (1 cup) of prepared, chopped fresh fruit (see suggestions below) with 125ml (½ cup) each of yoghurt and cold milk, together with 1 tbsp honey, sugar or silan (date syrup) and a little bit of crushed ice. Alternately, use frozen fruit instead of fresh fruit and ice. Simply blend together until smooth and serve at once.

Here are some combinations of fruit and flavourings I like to use:

STRAWBERRY:
200g (7oz) strawberries, halved

PINEAPPLE AND MINT:
200g (7oz) cubed fresh pineapple and 4 mint leaves

BANANA AND DATE:
1 ripe banana, 1 pitted date, a pinch of ground cinnamon or cardamom

I like to give my sons fresh fruit smoothies in the morning as a great start to their day. They are very simple to make if you have a blender.

Sweet Memories

גלידה

THE KIOSK

On the way home from school, on the edges of the market, there was a tiny kiosk (shop). One hot summer my kind parents allowed me to buy cold drinks and ice lollies there on credit. 'You can have a sweet as well, from time to time,' they said. For me, 'from time to time' meant 'all the time!' I was thrilled. I felt like Bilbi (the Hebrew name for Pippi Longstocking). I would come every day and try all my favourite sweets: black liquorice we used to call 'Sus', Bananit (banana sweets), Krembo, Shalva (a sweet puffed wheat snack), Tropit drink. Everything I could dream of was there to be enjoyed. For free!

News spread about my account. Knowing that I was a generous girl, my whole class 'volunteered', each one in turn, to escort me home.... After a few months, my poor father had to pay the bill (big time). I thought he was going to be angry but instead he took me straight to the dentist to check my teeth!

Samis' Grocery store

MUM'S TORTE CAKE

MAKES ONE 24CM (9½ IN) CAKE

6 eggs, at room temperature, separated
1 tbsp lemon juice
1 tbsp oil
200g (1 cup) sugar
140g (1 cup) flour

FOR THE YELLOW AND PINK CREAMS
500ml (2 cups) whipping cream
90g (3oz) Vanilla Instant Pudding*
250ml (1 cup) milk
4–6 tbsp sugar
Red food colouring

*In Israel in the 1970s a lot of cake recipes added vanilla pudding mixture rather than crème patissière to cream, as using raw eggs in the heat wouldn't have been safe.

Preheat the oven to 180°C/350°F. Grease and base-line a 24cm (9½ in) round cake tin.

Make the cake: Place the egg yolks in a small bowl, pour over the lemon juice and oil and set aside.

Using a stand mixer, whisk the egg whites with the sugar until stiff peaks form. Reduce the beater speed to minimum and gradually add in the egg yolk mixture. Add the flour and gently fold in. Place in the prepared tin and bake for 30 minutes until set and risen. Test that the cake is cooked through by piercing its centre with a skewer; if it comes out clean, the cake is ready. Set aside to cool on a wire rack.

Make the yellow cream: In a stand mixer, whisk together 250ml (1 cup) whipping cream, 45g (1½ oz) Vanilla Instant Pudding, 125ml (½ cup) milk and 2–3 tbsp sugar until it comes together to form a fluffy cream. Remove and reserve.

Make the pink cream: Add the remaining cream, Vanilla Instant Pudding, milk and sugar along with a few drops of red food colouring to the stand mixer bowl and whisk until it forms a pink fluffy cream.

Halve the cooled cake. Top the bottom half of the cake with a layer of pink cream, reserving some for decoration, then sandwich with the remaining cake half. Decorate the top and sides with the yellow cream. Pipe on the remaining pink cream in swirls to decorate. Serve at once or cover it and store in the fridge until serving.

This is a cake my mother first made over 40 years ago. She is an excellent baker and I always loved her cakes. One day at a friend's house I saw a torte cake with two colours, pink and yellow, something I'd never seen before. I was amazed! I went home and told my mother and a few days later she had created this lovely layered cake for me.

CHOCOLATE ROULADE

MAKES ONE 35CM (14 IN) LONG ROULADE

45g (⅓ cup) flour
35g (¼ cup) cocoa
1 tsp baking powder
Pinch of salt
4 eggs at room temperature, separated
100g (½ cup) caster (superfine) sugar
1 tsp vanilla essence
Icing (confectioners) sugar, for sprinkling

VANILLA FILLING
250ml (1 cup) whipping cream
125ml (½ cup) milk
30g (3 tbsp) Vanilla Instant Pudding

Preheat the oven to 190°C/375°F. Line a 30cm x 40cm (12in x16in) baking tray with lightly oiled baking parchment.

Make the roulade: Sift the flour and cocoa into a bowl. Stir in the baking powder and salt.

In stand mixer, whisk the egg whites with 50g (¼ cup) caster (superfine) sugar until firm peaks form. Remove and reserve.

In the same mixer bowl, place the egg yolks, remaining sugar and vanilla essence. Whisk until pale and fluffy. Reduce the speed to minimum. Gradually add the flour mixture. Using a spatula, lightly fold in half the whisked egg white, then fold in the remaining egg white.

Place the mixture on the baking tray and spread evenly. Bake for 12 minutes until set.

Sprinkle icing (confectioners) sugar generously over a clean kitchen towel. Invert the baked chocolate sponge onto the towel. Carefully peel off the baking parchment from its base.

Using the towel, carefully roll up the warm cake lengthways. Leave to cool completely.

Prepare the filling: Whisk together all the filling ingredients to form a firm cream.

Carefully unroll the roulade. Spread evenly with the vanilla cream filling. Roll back into roulade shape and trim the edges. Cover and chill for at least 1 hour before serving.

Chocolate roulade was another star of the '70s. It was made using either a vanilla or chocolate sponge, with the filling always in a contrasting colour. This chocolate roulade is deliciously light and makes a wonderful dessert, guaranteed to transport people of a certain age back to their childhoods!

BASBOUSA

MAKES 24 PORTIONS

CAKE
600g (3 cups) coarse semolina
200g (1 cup) sugar
500g (1lb 2oz) sour cream, at room temperature
100g (3½ oz) desiccated coconut
200g (7oz) unsalted butter, melted
2 tsp baking powder
1 tsp vanilla essence

DECORATION
24 blanched almonds

SUGAR SYRUP
400g (2 cups) sugar
500ml (2 cups) water
2 tbsp orange blossom water or rose water

Preheat the oven to 180°C/350°F. Butter a 25 x 35cm (10 x 14in) rimmed baking tray.

Make the cake: In a bowl, thoroughly mix together all the cake ingredients with your hands or a large whisk. Place the mixture in the buttered tray, pressing down firmly and smoothing the surface. With a sharp knife, score into 24 squares. Place an almond in the centre of each square, pressing it in slightly.

Bake for 30–40 minutes until golden brown.

Make the syrup: Meanwhile, boil the sugar and water in a saucepan over medium heat for 5 minutes, until the sugar has dissolved and the mixture thickened. Stir in the orange blossom water. Leave to cool thoroughly.

Add the syrup: Remove the freshly baked cake from the oven and slice through the scored lines. Using a large spoon, pour all the syrup gradually and evenly over the hot cake. Leave to cool completely before serving.

This will keep for two days at room temperature or 10 days covered in the fridge.

My mother found this recipe in a newspaper published after Anwar al Sadat visited Israel in 1977. Originally from Egypt, this cake is found all over the Middle East. The semolina soaks up the syrup, making it wonderfully soft and juicy. The name 'basbousa' means 'only a kiss', but it's a kiss you want more of! I make this for special occasions and like to serve it with sour cream on the side, as a tangy contrast to the cake.

CHEESE DELKALACH

MAKES 20 SMALL DELKALACH OR 2 PLAITED DELKALACH

DOUGH

25g (1oz) fresh yeast or 2½ tsp of dried
100g (½ cup) sugar
480g (3½ cups) strong bread flour
Up to 250ml (1 cup) hand-hot milk
2 large eggs plus 1 egg yolk, lightly beaten together
Grated zest of 1 lemon (optional)
150g (5oz) butter, melted
227g (8oz) tub sour cream
Pinch of salt

FILLING

500g (1lb 2oz) full-fat soft cheese (curd cheese) or cream cheese
140g (⅔ cup) sugar
2 egg yolks
2 tbsp cornflour (corn starch)
1 tbsp Vanilla Instant Pudding (optional)
2 tsp vanilla essence
Grated zest of 1 lemon

1 egg, beaten, to glaze

Icing (confectioners) sugar, to decorate

TIP: For the filling I like to use full-fat Longley Farm or Farmer Cheese.

Make the dough: Crumble the yeast into the bowl of a stand mixer, or sprinkle in if using dried. Add 1 tbsp sugar, 1 tbsp flour and 5 tbsp milk. Mix with a spoon, cover and set aside for 15 minutes until the mixture has become frothy and formed a head. Add 400g (3 cups) flour, the remaining sugar and beaten egg then begin mixing together with the dough hook. Gradually, add in the butter a tbsp at a time, mixing well with each addition. Then mix in the sour cream. The dough should be soft and slightly sticky (if required, add more of the hand-hot milk). Add in the salt and mix in.

At a low speed, mix for 5–6 minutes until the dough begins to pull away from the sides of the bowl. If the dough does not pull away, add in the remaining flour and mix in well until it does come away from the sides. You want the dough to be soft, supple and slightly sticky.

Keeping the dough in the bowl, sprinkle over a little flour and cover with film. Place in the fridge to rise slowly for at least 6 hours or overnight.

Make the filling: In a mixing bowl, mix together all the filling ingredients until combined.

Shape and fill the delkalach: First, line two baking trays with baking parchment. Divide the dough into two even portions. On a lightly floured surface, roll out one portion of the dough (leaving the other covered) to form a square 5mm (¼in) thick. For the small delkalach, cut the square into 8cm (3in) squares.

Place a teaspoon of the filling in the centre of a pastry square. Bring together the two diagonally opposite pastry corners up over the filling, twisting them together. Now do the same with the other corners, making a parcel. Repeat the process until all the squares have been filled.

Carefully transfer the delkalach to the trays. Cover with a clean kitchen towel and set aside to rise for 30 minutes.

Use the remaining pastry and filling in the same way, setting aside to rise for 30 minutes.

Bake the delkalach: Preheat the oven to 190°C/375°F.

Check the risen delkalach. If the parcels have opened while rising, pinch the dough together to seal them. Brush with beaten egg and bake for 15 minutes until golden. As soon as they come out from the oven, dust with icing (confectioners) sugar and set aside to cool. Store in an airtight container for 3–4 days or freeze. Best of all though, is to eat them slightly warm from the oven!

Alternatively, for the plaited delkalach: Divide the dough into two even portions and roll out each portion into a 25 x 35cm (10 x 14in) rectangle, around 5mm (¼in) thick. Take one rectangle and place half the filling mixture in a line down the centre, leaving a gap at each end. Cut slightly diagonal 2cm-wide cuts (around ¾ in) in the dough on either side of the filling. Fold the top of the dough up over the filling, then braid the pastry strips, finally folding over the bottom of the dough to form a parcel. Cover with a clean kitchen towel, set aside to rise for 30 minutes. Repeat the process with the remaining dough. Glaze both the plaited delkalach with beaten egg and bake for 25 minutes until golden. Dust with icing (confectioners) sugar as soon as they come out of the oven.

TIP: For an alternative topping, sprinkle Streusel (see p.391) over the top once you've brushed it with beaten egg and then bake it.

You can't beat the Hungarians when it comes to pastries! One of my favourites is delkalach, made from pillows of yeast dough with a sweet cheese filling inside. In Israel, it's so popular that it's widely sold in shops, but home-made is the best!

HONEY CAKE

MAKES 2 CAKES

150g (¾ cup) sugar
1 level tbsp cocoa
½ tsp ground cloves
1 tsp cinnamon
¼ tsp ground cardamom (optional)
Pinch of salt

COFFEE

1 tsp ground coffee
180ml (¾ cup) boiling water

WET INGREDIENTS

¾ cup* 180ml (6 fl oz) honey
¼ cup* (4 tbsp) smooth strawberry jam
125ml (½ cup) oil
2 eggs

DRY INGREDIENTS

315g (2¼ cups) flour
1 level tsp bicarbonate of soda

TOPPING

Flaked almonds or chopped walnut pieces

*For this traditional recipe, I'm preserving the original cup measurements, which work so well for measuring honey and jam. If preferred, you can omit the jam, using 1 cup of honey instead.

In a stand mixer bowl, place the sugar, cocoa, cloves, cinnamon, cardamom and salt. Mix together using a spoon until there no lumps.

Make the coffee: Stir the coffee and boiling water in a cup until thoroughly dissolved. Add it quickly to the ingredients in the bowl and mix together using a spoon until the sugar melts.

Add the wet ingredients: In a separate bowl, beat the wet ingredients together and add to the mixer bowl. Use the mixer whisk at a medium speed to mix together well.

Add the dry ingredients: Whisk in the dry ingredients until well mixed. Cover the mixture with film and refrigerate for at least 6 hours or overnight.

Bake the cakes: Preheat the oven to 140°C/275°F. Oil two 10 x 20cm (4 x 8 in) rectangular cake tins*.

Lightly fold the chilled cake mixture. Divide it among the two cake tins. Sprinkle the nuts on top.

Bake the cakes in the oven for 1¼ hours. Test that they are cooked through by inserting a skewer into the centre of each cake; if it comes out clean, the cakes are ready.

*I also like to bake it in a ring mould cake tin.

Honey cakes are eaten for the Jewish New Year to ensure a sweet year ahead. I've eaten a lot of honey cakes and this one is the best! It's based on a recipe given to me by a friend 20 years ago, which I've spent a lot of time working on and adapting. It's a wonderfully fragrant cake which keeps very well and can also be frozen. My advice is make triple quantities of it — in my family, this honey cake vanishes as quickly as I make it!

ENGLISH CAKE

MAKES 1 CAKE

PEEL MIXTURE

- 2–3 drops of rum essence
- 70ml (¼ cup) hot water
- 2 tbsp raisins
- 120g (4oz) assorted chopped candied peel
- ½ tbsp flour

CAKE

- 125g (½ cup) unsalted butter, softened
- 100g (½ cup) sugar
- 1 tsp vanilla essence
- 2 eggs
- 140g (1 cup) flour
- 1 tsp baking powder
- Pinch of salt
- Grated zest of 1 lemon (optional)

Preheat oven to 170°C/340°F. Grease and base line one 6 x 10 x 25cm (2½ x 4 x 10in) loaf tin

Prepare the peel mixture: Add the rum essence to the hot water, add the raisins and soak for 10 minutes. Drain thoroughly, mix with the candied peel and set aside.

Make the cake: Place the butter and sugar and vanilla essence in the bowl of a stand mixer with a K beater. Using a medium-high speed, mix until fluffy, around 2 minutes. Add the eggs, one at a time, mixing between each addition and scraping the mixture from the sides to ensure it is thoroughly mixed.

Sift together the flour, baking powder and salt. At a low speed, mix in half of the flour mixture, then use a spatula to fold in the remaining flour and lemon zest.

Toss the peel mixture with ½ tbsp flour, to help prevent it from clumping together and sinking. At a slow speed, mix in half the peel mixture into the cake mix.

Place the cake mixture in the cake tin, spreading it in evenly. Now top with the remaining peel mixture, sprinkling it on evenly.

Place the cake in the oven. Bake for 45 minutes until golden. Check as it bakes; if browning too quickly, reduce the oven temperature to 150°C/300°F.

Test if the cake is ready by inserting a skewer in to the centre of the cake. If it comes out clean and dry, the cake is cooked through. Remove and cool.

In Israel, English Cake is found in every household and served in hotels for Saturday morning breakfast. Indeed it's so popular that we have specific, rectangular cake tins called 'English cake tins'. So, naturally, when I came to England, I was looking forward to enjoying the best English Cake ever. Instead, I discovered that none of the English bakeries here knew what I was talking about! When I investigated, I found out that the English Cake we enjoy in Israel is a 'souvenir' of the British presence in the Middle East. It's a version of the Madeira cake, which the French call cake Anglais, enriched with candied peel and raisins. So, now I offer my English and American readers this recipe for an Israeli English Cake!

BAKED CREAM SLICES

MAKES ONE 25 X 35CM (10 X 14IN) TRAYFUL

DOUGH

400g (3 cups) self-raising flour
200g (⅞ cup) unsalted butter, softened
120g (½ cup plus 1 tbsp) sugar
1 tsp vanilla essence
4 egg yolks

JAM LAYER

320g (1¼ cup) smooth strawberry or apricot jam

TOPPING

4 egg whites
100g (½ cup) sugar
80g (2¾ oz) Vanilla Instant Pudding
50g (2oz) dark chocolate, coarsely grated

Preheat the oven to 180°C/350°F. Butter a 25 x 35cm (10 x 14in) rimmed baking tray.

Make the dough: Place the flour, butter, sugar and vanilla essence in the bowl of a stand mixer. Using the K paddle, mix together slowly. Add the yolks and mix at medium speed until the mixture forms a smooth dough.

Take out a third of the dough, cover with film and chill in the fridge.

Bake the dough and add the jam layer: Place the dough in the baking tray and, using your fingers, press it out to form a thin, even layer that lines the tray. Bake for 10 minutes until set, remove, allow to cool completely, then spread evenly with the jam.

Add the topping and bake: Preheat the oven to 180°C/350°F. Whisk the egg whites with the sugar until stiff. Fold in the Vanilla Instant Pudding gently but thoroughly.

Spread the whisked egg white evenly over the jam. Sprinkle over half of the grated chocolate.

Take the chilled dough and coarsely grate it in an even layer over the top. Sprinkle with the remaining chocolate.

Bake for 20 minutes until the crumble is nicely golden.

Remove, cool and slice as desired into squares or rectangles.

This tray-bar bake offers a wonderful combination of textures and flavours: a crisp base, a touch of jam and soft, light, vanilla meringue — while the crumbly dough and chocolate topping is the glorious finishing touch to this treat.

HAPPY BIRTHDAY

BIRTHDAYS

I couldn't wait for birthday parties as a child. I can't tell you how excited I felt.

The parties followed a satisfying pattern. Every mother baked a birthday cake. For some reason, it was always chocolate cake covered with icing, topped with colourful sprinkles and candles. The birthday boy or girl would wear a crown made from carnations. There were balloons, little gifts for the guests and lots of birthday songs.

The birthday presents were modest -a new colouring set, plasticine or a pencil case — but we were thrilled to get them. The food was typical '70s: sliced vegetable crudités with dip, halved pittas with hummus and pickles or salami, sweets, fizzy drinks and ice lollies (ice pops).

We played games together instead of sitting to watch an entertainer: Candle in the Bottle, Musical Chairs, Bingo, True or False. We would dance in a circle, holding hands or with arms entwined. I can still hum the tunes we danced to.

Following the cake and the lifting of the birthday boy or girl onto a chair, each guest received a goodie bag of sweets and a small gift like an eraser or a whistle at the end of the party.

I throw birthday parties for my sons which follow this same pattern, though they refuse to wear a carnation crown! I prepare lots of balloons, home-made chocolate cake, their favourite foods, fizzy drinks (the one time of year they can drink sodas), and we play games together — simple pleasures which we enjoy as a family.

70s BIRTHDAY CAKE

MAKES ONE LARGE CAKE

400g (2 cups) sugar
65g (⅔ cup) cocoa powder
160ml (⅔ cup) water
170g (5½ oz) unsalted butter
6 eggs, at room temperature, separated
Pinch of salt
180g (1⅓ cup) flour
7g (¾ tbsp) baking powder

CHOCOLATE GANACHE ICING
(for an alternative icing see Basics, p.391)
250ml (1 cup) whipping cream
250g (9oz) dark chocolate, in pieces

Sprinkles, to decorate

Make the cake: Place 300g (1½ cup) sugar, cocoa powder, water and butter in a saucepan. Cook, stirring, over a very low heat, until the sugar dissolves and the butter melts to form a chocolate syrup. Set aside to cool slightly.

Preheat to the oven to 170°C/340°F. Thoroughly grease a large cake tin — the ideal size is 23 x 37cm (9 x 15in).

Using a stand mixer, whisk the egg whites with the remaining sugar and a pinch of salt until stiff peaks form. Reduce the mixer speed to minimum and add the egg yolks, one at a time.

Mix the flour and baking powder. Gradually add to the egg mixture, mixing in well.

With the mixer still going, slowly pour in the chocolate syrup, mixing it in well. Once this has been added in, stop the mixer and fold together to make sure everything is well mixed.

Transfer the mixture to the baking pan, spreading evenly. Tap the tin firmly on your work surface a few times to remove any bubbles.

Bake for around 30–35 minutes until set. Test with a skewer; if it comes out clean the cake is ready. Allow it to cool.

Make the chocolate ganache: icing Place the cream in a saucepan and heat over medium heat. When it's almost come to the boil, turn off the heat. Add the chocolate and whisk together briskly until the chocolate melts and combines to form a thick, smooth chocolatey mixture.

Pour the warm ganache evenly over the top and sides of the cake. Let it cool slightly and then decorate with sprinkles.

This cake was an essential part of growing up in Israel in the '70s. Every kid at kindergarten got this cake for their birthday — that's how it was. Today, even when I make fancier chocolate cakes, this simple, satisfying cake is the one my kids want most!

Happy
HAPPY

CHOCOLATE COCONUT CAKE

MAKES ONE 23CM (9IN) CAKE

6 eggs, at room temperature, separated
300g (1½ cups) sugar

DRY INGREDIENTS
140g (1 cup) self-raising flour
100g (1 cup) chopped walnuts
100g (3½ oz) dark chocolate, coarsely grated
100g (1 cup) desiccated coconut

WET INGREDIENTS
125ml (½ cup) oil
125ml (½ cup) freshly squeezed orange juice
1 tbsp sour cream (optional)

Limi's Chocolate Icing (see p.391)

Desiccated coconut, for sprinkling

Preheat the oven to 160°C/325°F. Grease a 23cm (9in) square tin.

Using a stand mixer, whisk the egg whites until soft peaks form, then gradually add 200g (1 cup) sugar, whisking all the time, until stiff peaks form.

In a mixing bowl, mix together all the dry ingredients with the remaining sugar.

In a separate bowl, mix the wet ingredients. If you want the cake to be extra soft, stir in the sour cream.

Now add the mixed wet ingredients to the dry ingredients and use a hand whisk to mix well. Add the egg yolks, one at a time, mixing in well between each addition.

Mix a third of the whisked egg whites into the cake mix to loosen it. Gently but thoroughly fold in the remaining whisked egg.

Transfer to the cake tin, level it out and bake for 30–40 minutes until set. Test with a skewer; if it comes out clean, the cake is ready.

Set the cake aside to cool. Make the chocolate icing and use it to top the cake. Decorate with desiccated coconut. Cut the cake into squares and serve.

This cake was a star of my childhood Shabbats, as my mother made it for us almost every week. The chocolate icing is my addition to this family recipe, making the cake richer and even more of a treat!

LIMI'S CARROT CAKE

MAKES ONE 20CM (8IN) SQUARE) CAKE

DRY INGREDIENTS

300g (10oz) carrots (about 4 medium carrots), peeled and finely grated
200g (1 cup) caster (superfine) sugar*
210g (1½ cup) flour
¼ tsp salt
2 tsp baking powder
¼ tsp bicarbonate of soda
1 tsp ground ginger
1 tsp ground cinnamon
¼ tsp ground cloves
100g (¾ cup) raisins
2 tbsp walnut pieces

WET INGREDIENTS

3 eggs
3 tbsp oil
1 tbsp sour cream
1 tsp vanilla essence

CARROT HALWA TOPPING (OPTIONAL)

20g (2 tbsp) butter
2 tbsp sugar
5 tbsp full-fat milk
2 carrots, coarsely grated
A pinch of freshly ground cardamom (optional)

CREAM CHEESE FROSTING

50g (4 tbsp) unsalted butter, softened
250g (9oz) cream cheese
½ tsp vanilla essence
4 tbsp icing (confectioners) sugar

TIP: I like to use a 50/50 mixture of white and golden sugar

Preheat the oven to 180°C/350°F. Grease a 20 x 20cm (8 x 8in) cake tin.

Make the cake: In a large bowl, mix all the dry ingredients by hand until the moisture is released from carrots and the mixture feels moist.

In a separate bowl, whisk all the wet ingredients until thoroughly mixed.

Add the wet ingredients to the dry ones and whisk together.

Transfer the mixture to the cake tin, smooth the surface, and bake for 40 minutes to 1 hour. Allow the cake to cool completely.

While the cake is baking, make the halwa if using: Melt the butter in a frying pan over medium heat. Mix in the sugar and milk. Add the carrot, mixing well. Cook, stirring now and then, until most of the liquid has been absorbed and the carrot is softened and caramelised. Stir in the cardamom if using. Set aside to cool.

Cream cheese frosting: Thoroughly mix together the ingredients.

Assemble the cake: Slice the cake across into two halves. Spread half of the cream cheese frosting over the bottom cake half and top with the other cake half. Spread the remaining frosting over the top. Decorate with carrot halwa, if using.

I first encountered carrot cake when I came to England. The spices in it reminded me of Jewish honey cake and I set to work experimenting with recipes, until I made a version I was happy with. I came up with the carrot topping after I'd been to an Indian restaurant and eaten carrot halwa there. I thought at once that it would make a wonderful topping for carrot cake. Not only does it look striking, it adds an extra dimension of carrot flavour and texture.

I ❤
TEL AVIV

TEL AVIV
ME

GRANDMA'S ORANGE CAKE

MAKES ONE 24CM (9½ IN) CAKE

CAKE
200g (1 cup) sugar
4 eggs at room temperature
Pinch of salt
1 tsp vanilla essence
Zest of 2 oranges
250ml (1 cup) freshly squeezed orange juice
175ml (6 fl oz) oil
280g (2 cups) self-raising flour

GLAZE
175g (1⅓ cup) icing (confectioners) sugar
2–3 tbsp boiling water
Zest of 1 orange

Candied orange peel, for decoration

Preheat the oven to 170°C/340°F. Grease a 24cm (9½ in) round cake tin.

Make the cake: Using a stand mixer at a high speed, whisk together the sugar, eggs, salt, vanilla essence and orange zest for 2–3 minutes until it forms a foamy mass. In a separate bowl, whisk together the orange juice and oil. Reduce the mixer speed to low and add the orange juice mixture in a thin stream, mixing well. Fold in the flour well.

Transfer the cake mixture to the greased cake tin, spreading it evenly. Bake for 40 minutes. Use a skewer to test the cake; if it comes out clean, the cake is ready. If the top of the cake is brown but the inside is not yet cooked, reduce the heat to 150°C/300°F and bake for a further 10–15 minutes. Remove and cool on a rack.

Prepare the glaze: Mix the glaze ingredients together to form a soft, slightly runny paste. Use a spoon to spread it evenly all over the cake. Decorate with candied orange peel and serve. Store at room temperature.

Orange cakes have a tendency to collapse, so it's hard to find one that keeps its shape nicely. I discovered this recipe — which in Israel is known as 'Grandma's Orange Cake' — which always works a treat. My mother had another recipe she used to use, until I gave her this one to try. Now this version has become her go-to 'juice cake' recipe.

NOSTALGIC STRAWBERRY JELLY SQUARES

MAKES ONE 22CM (9IN) SQUARE CAKE

CAKE

4 eggs, at room temperature, separated
140g (⅔ cup) sugar
1 tsp oil
1 tsp lemon juice
90g (⅔ cup) flour

SYRUP

250ml (1 cup) syrup from a can of canned pineapple
1–2 tbsp sugar

CREAM

250ml (1 cup) whipping cream
80g (2¾ oz) Vanilla Instant Pudding
125ml (½ cup) milk
2 tbsp sugar

TOPPING

18–20 strawberries, halved
1 x 135g strawberry jelly cubes or 1 x 85g (3oz) sachet of strawberry jelly (Jello-O) powder

Preheat the oven to 180°C/350°F. Grease a 22cm (9in) square cake tin.

Make the cake: Using a stand mixer, whisk the egg whites until soft peaks form, then gradually add the sugar, whisking all the time, until stiff peaks form.

Place the egg yolks in a bowl and pour over the oil and lemon juice.

Reduce the mixer speed to minimum, add in the egg yolk mixture a quarter at a time, whisking well between each addition. Gradually add half the flour, mixing well. Stop the mixer and fold in the remaining flour with a spatula

Transfer the cake mix to the tin and bake for 25–30 minutes. Test with a skewer; if it comes out clean, the cake is cooked through. Remove from the oven and allow to cool.

Make the syrup: Once the cake has cooled, gently heat together the pineapple syrup and 1 tbsp sugar. Bring to the boil and taste to check the sweetness. Add more sugar if wanted. Allow the syrup to cool slightly.

Slice the cake in half across. Using a tbsp, drizzle some of the syrup on each cake half so as to moisten it slightly.

Prepare the cream: Whisk all the ingredients together until they are thick and fluffy.

Spread half the cream over the bottom half of the cake. Sandwich with the other cake half. Spread the remaining cream in a layer over the top of the cake.

Add the topping: Arrange the strawberries cut side down in a neat layer on top of the cream. Cover and chill in the fridge.

Whisk the jelly (Jell-O) in 500ml (2 cups) of boiling water until dissolved. Whisk for further 2 minutes to cool it slightly, then spoon it over the strawberries to form a jelly layer which covers the fruit. Cool slightly, then chill in the fridge before serving.

Every child loves strawberries, jelly (Jell-O) and cream — so what better treat than combining them all in one glorious cake!

EASY NUT TORTE

MAKES ONE 22CM (9IN) CAKE

CAKE
6 eggs, at room temperature, separated
200g (1 cup) sugar
100g (¾ cup) self-raising flour
100g (1 cup) ground walnuts

FILLING
250ml (1 cup) whipping cream
2 tbsp sugar

Limi's Chocolate Icing (see p.391)

8 walnut halves, to decorate

Preheat oven to 180°C/350°F. Grease a 22cm (9in) cake tin.

Make the cake: Using a stand mixer, whisk the egg whites until soft peaks form, then gradually add the sugar, whisking all the time, until stiff peaks form.

In a separate bowl, mix the flour and ground walnuts.

Reduce the speed to minimum and add the egg yolks, one at a time, mixing between each addition. Gradually add the flour mixture until everything is mixed well.

Transfer to the cake tin and level the mixture. Bake for 25–30 minutes until set. Test with a skewer; if it comes out clean, the cake is ready.

While the cake is baking, make the icing.

Cool the cake on a rack.

Make the filling: Once it is cool, whip together the filling ingredients into a fluffy cream. Carefully slice the cake across in half. Top the bottom cake half with the filling and sandwich with the remaining half.

Spread the icing evenly over the top and sides and decorate with the walnut halves. Store in the fridge until serving.

"A very simple cake to make. Rich and nutty, this comes with chocolate and cream to make the sin complete!"

CRUMB CHEESECAKE

MAKES ONE 26CM (10½ IN) CHEESECAKE

PASTRY

200g (1 cup) softened unsalted butter
2 egg yolks
3 tbsp sugar
280g (2 cups) self-raising flour

FILLING

200g (1 cup) sugar
227g (8oz) tub sour cream
500ml whipping cream
80g (2¾ oz) Vanilla Instant Pudding
1 tsp vanilla essence
250g (9oz) full-fat soft cheese
250g (9oz) reduced-fat soft cheese

Make and bake the pastry: Preheat the oven to 180°C/350°F. Generously butter a 26cm (10½ in) springform round cake tin, especially the base and line a baking tray.

Using a stand mixer with a K-paddle, mix all the pastry ingredients until thoroughly mixed.

For the pastry base, take half of the pastry and press it firmly into the base of the cake tin to form a 2mm (around ¹⁄₁₆ in) even layer. Prick thoroughly with a fork to keep it from rising.

For the crumble topping, take the remaining pastry and press it out very finely to the same thickness on a lined baking tray.

Bake both pastries for around 15–20 minutes, until golden. Remove and cool completely. Set aside the base in the cake tin. Take the pastry on the baking tray and crumble this with your fingers into fine crumbs, to use as a topping.

Make the filling: Place all the ingredients apart from the cheese in a stand mixer. Use the whisk to whisk together until the cream is whipped and the mixture is light and smooth. Add in the cheese and whisk again until well mixed.

Assemble the cheesecake: Spoon the filling onto the pastry base in the cake tin. Sprinkle a 1cm (⅓in) layer of the pastry crumbs evenly over the top. Any leftover crumbs can be stored in an airtight container and frozen for future use.

Cover and chill overnight before serving so that it sets.

This light-textured crumb cheesecake is the most popular of all Israeli cheesecakes. It's simple to make and, as it should be prepared in advance, is perfect for entertaining.

Shalom Goodbye

NOVEMBER OF 1977

It was a sunny morning in Tel Aviv. I was seven years old, walking to school with my neighbour's son Gadi Polak. He was a year older than me. I liked to walk with him. He made me laugh with his Donald Duck impressions. As we walked, I thought about November. I didn't know that it could be so beautiful. It was not a month that I'd thought much about before. It comes after summer, before winter and passes by quietly.

As we walked through Carmel Market, I smelled something different in the air. November had brought a sweet scent of hope because the day before, the President of Egypt Anwar Sadat had come to Israel.

In honour of his visit, my school asked the pupils to write about the coming peace. My assignment was chosen for the school newspaper. I wrote:

> *'When peace will come I will go to Egypt. I will see Pharaoh's palace, the Nile where little Moses was found and the beautiful pyramids. From Egypt I will travel to the Red Sea where Moses and the sons of Israel passed through. On the way I might see their footsteps...'*

Gadi asked if I would really go to Egypt. 'I don't know,' I said, 'maybe just to see the Pyramids.'

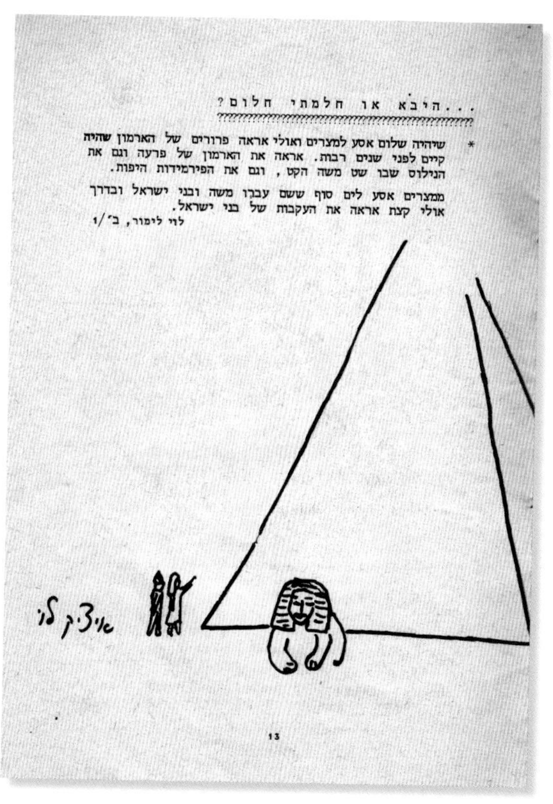

...היבא או חלמתי חלום?

* שיהיה שלום אסע למצרים ואולי אראה פרורים של הארמון שהיה קיים לפני שנים רבות. אראה את הארמון של פרעה וגם את הנילוס שבו שט משה הקט, וגם את הפירמידות היפות.

ממצרים אסע לים סוף ששם עברו משה ובני ישראל ובדרך אולי קצת אראה את העקבות של בני ישראל.

לוי לימור, ב׳/1

13

I passed through Allenby Street (named after the British Field Marshal Viscount Allenby). In those days Allenby Street had the best fashion stores in town. I was impressed by one shop in particular, full of dazzling evening gowns. I stood outside, imagining how I would look in each one of them.

Just before I got to The Balfour School, I passed a small yard covered with little yellow flowers called 'Savyonim' in Hebrew (a type of groundsel). I knew that winter had arrived when they appeared. I was delighted to see them. It felt like they wished me a good day.

PEACE CAKE

MAKES ONE ROULADE AROUND 30CM (12IN) LONG

BISCUIT ROULADE

360ml (1½ cups) milk
3½ tbsp cocoa
200g (1 cup) softened butter
120g (⅔ cup) icing (confectioners) sugar
450g (1lb) vanilla flavour petit beurre biscuits

CREAM FILLING

375ml (1½ cups) whipping cream
190ml (6½ fl oz) milk
100g (3½ oz) Vanilla Instant Pudding
3–4 tbsp sugar

TIP: Some brands of kosher whipping cream can be very thick, in which case I use 250ml (1 cup) of milk instead of 190ml (6½ fl oz) to thin it.

Make the biscuit roulade: Bring the milk to the boil in a saucepan, then transfer to a bowl and leave to cool slightly.

In a large bowl, using a hand whisk, whisk together the cocoa, butter and icing (confectioners) sugar until well mixed.

Dip the biscuits into the warm milk for 1–2 seconds, then drop into the cocoa mixture. Carefully fold together with a large spoon, gently breaking the biscuits into the mixture.

Transfer the mixture to the centre of a large sheet of baking parchment, spreading to form a 25 x 35cm (10 x 14in) rectangle around 1cm (⅓in) thick.

Make the cream filling: Whisk the cream filling ingredients until thickened. Spread the mixture in a line lengthways in the centre of the biscuit rectangle.

Lift up the two long sides of the parchment and carefully fold the biscuit mixture up over the filling, using the parchment to gently push the two halves together until they just meet. Pull the parchment tight, fold it over and seal it along the top of the cake with safety pins. Place it on a long tray and chill overnight. To serve, simply unwrap and cut into slices.

When Egypt's President Anwar Sadat visited Israel in 1977 as part of the peace process, there was huge excitement as he was the first Arab leader to visit Israel. I was only seven years old but I still vividly remember how everyone in the neighbourhood, including my family, came out onto their balconies and, as his plane flew overhead, we cheered and waved our flags. For the next Shabbat morning, to celebrate this historic event, my mother made this special roulade that I called 'Peace Cake'. It's very simple but it tastes AMAZING — for me it will always be the most delicious cake, leaving me with a sweet taste of PEACE.

OCTOBER 1981

The autumn of 1981 was a period of change. President Anwar Sadat of Egypt was assassinated in October. I was heartbroken. How could they take away a little girl's dream? A few months later, we sold our beloved home in Ezrah Hasofer. My parents moved us all to the suburbs north of Tel Aviv, which they felt would be a better, safer place to bring up the family.

I sat in the front of the moving truck and said goodbye to my home: to the living room with the orange curtains, to the balcony which faced the sea. Goodbye to my room with its pink curtains, to my mum's red and yellow kitchen. Goodbye to my neighbour Gadi and my friend Orit. Goodbye to the pitta bread bakery, the smells and colours of the market. Goodbye to the 'Savyonim'; I'll miss you, my little yellow flowers.

Goodbye Jaffa. Shalom to Ezrah Hasofer Street, to our time of peace.

I carry Tel Aviv in my heart though I live there no longer. My childhood instilled a lifelong sense of food and adventure. To this day I can still taste Tel Aviv.

יכין
Star Kist
קבוצת יבנה
5.50
6.-
8.-
8.50
9.-

Basics

SAVOURY BASICS

SOUP FOR COUSCOUS

MAKES AROUND 5–6 LITRES (5–6 QUARTS)

2 chicken legs, ideally from a roasting chicken, skinless
12 chicken wings
4 turkey necks

Oil for shallow-frying
3 carrots, peeled
A 500–600g (1lb 2oz–1lb–5oz) piece of pumpkin, skin on, but de-seeded
⅙ of a large white cabbage
1 courgette (zucchini), optional
1 onion, peeled
2 celery stalks with leaves attached
1 potato, peeled
2–3 garlic cloves, peeled
1 parsnip, peeled
A small handful of fresh dill
A handful of fresh parsley
A handful of fresh coriander
Sea salt
Pinch of ground turmeric
160g (5½ oz) cooked chickpeas (home-made or canned, rinsed and drained)

Couscous, to serve (see Two-stage Hand-rolled Couscous p.259 or Quick Couscous p.385).

Simmer the poultry: Place the poultry pieces in a large, deep saucepan. Cover with cold water and bring to the boil. Drain, discarding the water, so as to get rid of any impurities and excess fat. Rinse well in cold water and return to the pan. Add 6 litres (6 quarts) of water, cover and simmer gently over low heat for an hour.

Fry the vegetables: Towards the end of the simmering time, place oil in a large frying pan to lightly cover the surface and heat over a medium heat. Fry the carrots, pumpkin, courgette (zucchini), if using, and cabbage separately, until they're singed — lightly browned in places but not a uniform brown colour all over — and remove to a plate.

Complete cooking the soup: Add the fried vegetables with the remaining vegetables and herbs, apart from the chickpeas, to the simmered soup. Season with salt and turmeric, cover and simmer for a further hour. Add the chickpeas to the soup five minutes before the end of the cooking time.

Strain the soup, setting aside the poultry pieces and vegetables. From these, reserve only the chicken legs, turkey necks, vegetables, and chickpeas; discard the remainder.

To serve the couscous soup: Serve the couscous in a large round serving dish, surrounded by the vegetables and the poultry pieces with the soup on the side. This can be used to moisten the couscous to taste.

QUICK COUSCOUS

SERVES 4

450g (1lb) instant couscous
2 tbsp oil
1 tsp salt
625ml (2½ cups) boiling water

Place the couscous in a large saucepan and add the oil and salt. Using your hands, rub the grains to thoroughly coat them with the oil and salt.

Pour in the boiling water, stir lightly, cover tightly and set aside for 5 minutes. Uncover and use a fork to fluff up the couscous. Leave uncovered for another 5 minutes, fluff once more and serve at once.

LIMI'S RICE

SERVES 3

225g (1 cup) basmati rice
2–3 tbsp oil
Salt, according to taste
300ml (10 fl oz)285ml boiling water

Place the rice in a bowl, cover with cold water, gently stir with your hand and then rinse. Repeat the process twice more.

Heat a medium saucepan over medium heat. Add the oil and heat through. Add the rice and stir to coat with the oil.

Add the salt and mix in, then add the boiling water, stirring gently once or twice. Cover and bring to the boil, then reduce the temperature and cover the pan with two clean kitchen towels. Cook for 10 minutes. Turn off the heat and leave it to stand, covered, for a further 15 minutes until the water has been absorbed and the rice is cooked through. Fluff up the cooked rice with a fork and serve.

HUEVOS HAMINADOS

MAKES 6

6 eggs
2 brown onion skins

Place the eggs and onion skins in a saucepan and cover well with water. Bring to a simmer over medium-low heat, reduce the heat, and cook for 2–3 hours. This is the quick version. For eggs that are browner, simmer them for 6 hours.

These slow-cooked eggs are a traditional Sephardi dish, eaten as an accompaniment with Bourekas (see p.43) and Sabich (see p.23). Long simmering with the onion skins changes the colour of the eggs and gives them a deep, rich flavour.

FOCACCIA

MAKES 1 LOAF

DOUGH
500g (1lb 2oz) strong white flour
2 tsp dried instant yeast
4 tbsp olive oil, plus extra for brushing
1 tsp sugar
Around 300ml (10 fl oz) lukewarm water
1 heaped tsp salt

Pinch of semolina, for dusting

TOPPING
3 tbsp olive oil, plus extra for oiling
Coarse salt
Rosemary leaves

Make the dough: Place the flour and yeast in the bowl of a stand mixer. Make a well in the middle and add 3 tbsp olive oil and the sugar. Pour in 100ml (3½ fl oz) of the water. Using a dough hook mix at low speed for 2–5 minutes, gradually adding the remaining water. When the mixture has come together to form a dough, add the salt. Increase the speed slightly and mix for a further 5 minutes until the dough is smooth and supple.

Oil a bowl, take the dough and stretch it over itself from the top down (to help the gluten develop) and form it into a ball. Place in the oiled bowl. Cover with a clean kitchen towel and set aside to rise in a warm place for an hour.

Shape the focaccia: Oil a 30 x 40cm (12 x 16in) baking tray with olive oil and sprinkle a pinch of semolina on the surface.

Transfer the risen dough to the baking tray. Flatten to a rough rectangle or oval, around 2cm (¾in) thick. Press with your fingers to make dimples all over the surface of the dough and pour over 1 tbsp of olive oil. Cover loosely with cling film/plastic wrap and leave to rise for 40 minutes.

Preheat the oven to 200°C/400°F. Place an empty roasting pan in the bottom of the oven to heat through.

Dimple the risen dough again with your fingertips. For the topping, brush 2 tbsp olive oil over the dough into the holes. Sprinkle with coarse salt. Tuck a few rosemary leaves into the holes.

Bake the focaccia: Place the focaccia in the middle of the preheated oven. Pour boiling water into the preheated tin in the oven in order to create a steamy atmosphere as the loaf bakes. Bake for 25–30 minutes until golden. Remove and cool on a rack.

When I moved to London, I couldn't find focaccia in the kosher bakeries, so I taught myself how to make my own focaccia at home, in order to make Tuna Focaccia (see p.18)!

LIMI'S LAFFA

MAKES 10

50g fresh yeast or 5 tsp of dried
1 tbsp sugar
Around 400ml (1¾ cups) lukewarm water
1kg (2lb 4oz) strong flour
4 tbsp olive oil
1 tbsp salt

Make the dough: Crumble the fresh yeast, if using, into the bowl of a stand mixer; or just measure in the dried yeast. Add ½ tbsp sugar, 100ml (3½ fl oz) of lukewarm water and 1 tbsp of flour. Mix gently with a spoon and set aside to prove for 15 minutes until frothy.

Add the remaining sugar and flour and the olive oil. Mix with the dough hook at low speed for 3 minutes gradually adding 200ml (7 fl oz) of lukewarm water. Add the salt and mix for 6 minutes to form a soft, flexible, slightly sticky dough, adding more lukewarm water if needed.

Oil the dough and the bowl, and cover with a clean kitchen towel. Set aside for 1 hour, till risen and doubled in size.

Shape and cook the laffah: On a clean, oiled work surface, cut the dough into 10 equal-sized portions. Shape them into balls, place well apart on the oiled surface and leave for 20 minutes to rise.

Heat a flat griddle pan or large frying pan over a medium-high heat.

With oiled hands, take one portion of dough, flatten it to a 25cm (10in) circle and place on the hot griddle pan. Dry-fry for 1–2 minutes until flecked with brown patches underneath, then turn and cook on the other side for 1–2 minutes. Remove from the pan and cover with a clean kitchen towel to keep warm. Repeat the process, stacking them up as you cook them.

Serve warm or at room temperature. I use laffah for Sabich (see p.23) or Shawarma (see p.20). Once cool, they can be stored for one day in a plastic bag.

ZAHTAR PITTA

Cut out a circle from one side of a pitta, exposing the soft inside. Brush the inside with 1 tbsp olive oil and sprinkle with za'atar.

Place the pitta za'atar side downwards on a barbecue for half a minute until the pitta is charred, or grill it in the oven at 200°C/400°F for 1–2 minutes.

PUFFY FALAFEL CHIPS

2 large frying potatoes, peeled and finely sliced across
1 tsp salt
Oil for deep frying

BATTER
7 tbsp self-raising flour
1 tsp baking powder
2 eggs, beaten
½ tsp chicken stock powder
Pinch of black pepper

Soak the potato slices in cold water with 1 tsp salt for 30 minutes; drain and pat dry.

Make the batter by whisking together all the ingredients to form a smooth, thick, lump-free batter.

Heat the oil in a saucepan over medium-high heat. Once the oil is hot, reduce the heat to medium. Fry the falafel chips in batches Dip each potato slice briefly in the batter and drop at once into the hot oil. Fry until golden on both sides; remove with a slotted spoon and drain on kitchen paper. Serve at once with Falafel (see p.26).

PERFECT CHIPS

SERVES 5–6

1kg (2lb 4oz) frying potatoes*
Oil for deep frying
Salt to taste

* I use Maris Piper potatoes, but any potato variety that's good for frying will do.

Peel the potatoes and cut into fingers around 1.5cm (around ½ in) thick. Soak them in ice-cold water for 10–15 minutes, to wash off the excess starch. Drain and pat dry.

Pour oil for deep frying into a deep saucepan and heat over medium-high. Use the handle of a wooden spoon to test that the oil is hot. If bubbles form around it, the oil is ready.

Reduce the heat to medium and fry the chips (fries) in batches, so as not to overcrowd the pan, until lightly softened but still white, around 4 minutes. Remove and drain. Repeat the process until all the chips (fries) have been fried. Allow to cool, cover, and chill in the fridge for 30 minutes.

Heat the oil over a high heat. Fry in batches for a second time until golden. Drain well, season with salt, and serve at once.

CRISPY FRIED ONION

2 onions, halved lengthways and then sliced across
70g (½ cup) flour
Oil for frying

Coat the onion slices well with the flour, rubbing them with your hands to ensure they're thoroughly coated.

Pour oil to a depth of 2.5cm (1in) in a small saucepan and heat through over a medium heat. Fry handfuls of the onion in batches until golden-brown and crisp. Drain on kitchen paper and use as required.

PRESERVED LEMONS

MAKES 3

3 tbsp salt
½ tbsp sugar
3 lemons, sliced across around 5mm (¼in) thick
1 red chilli (optional)
Juice of 1–2 lemons

Mix the salt and sugar in a bowl. Lightly coat each lemon slice on both sides, shaking off the excess, and place in a preserving jar. Add the chilli if using.

Pour in enough lemon juice to cover the lemon slices and chilli. Seal the jar well. Set aside at room temperature for 2–3 days, then refrigerate for 2 days. The lemon slices are now ready to use and can be kept in the fridge for up to 2 months.

SWEET BASICS

SUGAR SYRUP

MAKES 300ML (1¼ CUP)

200g (1 cup) sugar
180ml (6½ fl oz) water
Juice of ½ lemon
1 tbsp orange blossom water (optional)

Place the sugar, water and lemon juice in a saucepan. Over a high heat, bring to the boil. Reduce the heat to medium and cook for 3–5 minutes to reduce slightly.

Remove from direct heat and stir in the orange blossom water, if using. Cool, cover, and chill for future use.

HOME-MADE CHOCOLATE RUGELACH FILLING

(MAKES ENOUGH TO FILL 64 RUGELACH)

400g (2 cups) sugar
200g (7oz, ¾ cup) margarine or butter, melted
175g (1¾ cups) cocoa powder
125ml (½ cup) vegetable oil
1 heaped tsp ground cinnamon

Mix together thoroughly until the sugar has dissolved and use to fill rugelach (see recipe p.165).

RICH BLINTZ FILLING

MAKES ENOUGH TO FILL 16 BLINTZES

Whisk 250ml (1 cup) dairy whipping cream with 1 heaped tbsp Vanilla Instant Pudding powder until fluffy. Fold it into 250g (9oz) soft white cheese sweetened with 3 tbsp sugar (see Blintzes recipe p.227).

STREUSEL

MAKES AROUND 300G

70g (½ cup) flour
150g (¾ cup) Demerara (soft brown) sugar
2 tbsp granulated sugar
75g (6 tbsp) cold butter
1 tsp vanilla essence

Mix everything in a stand mixer with a K-paddle until it resembles crumbs. Use for a topping as required.

LIMI'S CHOCOLATE ICING (NON-DAIRY)

MAKES ENOUGH TO ICE ONE CAKE

100ml (3½ fl oz) water
150g (5oz) dark chocolate, broken into squares
1 tbsp cocoa powder
3 tbsp sugar
1 tsp vanilla essence or 1 tbsp of your favourite liqueur
20g (2 tbsp) margarine

Place all ingredients apart from the margarine in a bain-marie, a heatproof bowl suspended over a saucepan of simmering water. Cook over a low heat, stirring constantly, until all the ingredients melt together, forming a smooth chocolate cream. Remove from direct heat, add the margarine and mix in until melted and glossy.

Cool slightly for 1–2 minutes, stir again, and use while still warm to ice your cake.

LIMI'S NOTES AND TIPS

- ❖ When deep frying, add a carrot to the oil as you heat it up. This keeps the oil nice and clear.
- ❖ To check whether the oil for deep frying is hot enough, place the handle of a wooden spoon in the oil. If bubbles form in a cluster around the handle, the oil is hot enough to begin frying.
- ❖ When coating a schnitzel, use one hand for dipping it into the beaten egg and the other hand for dipping it into the breadcrumbs. This keeps your hands from getting covered in sticky, eggy crumbs.
- ❖ When adding meatballs or fish balls to a sauce or soup, make sure the liquid is boiling when you put them in; this keeps them from falling apart.
- ❖ If a stew or soup is too salty, add 1 or 2 diced raw potatoes to soak up the excess salt and cook the dish for 15 minutes more. Discard the cooked potato if not needed in the dish.
- ❖ When I cook lentils, I always soak them in cold water for fifteen minutes first, then drain and rinse them before cooking as this makes them more digestible.
- ❖ When I cook dried pulses or grains such as rice or freekeh, I often use unsalted stock in place of water to give a richer flavour.
- ❖ When you make a soup from pulses, such as lentils or beans, add some fresh lemon juice at the end to enhance the flavour.
- ❖ A great way to heat up leftover cooked pasta is to place it in a sieve over the sink and pour over boiling water, then shake off any excess water.
- ❖ When I make a pie or a pizza, I like to pre-bake the pastry case or pizza base for 10–15 minutes to make sure it cooks through properly and ensure a good crisp texture.
- ❖ For best results when using puff pastry, start with a hot oven (200°C/400°F) until the pastry has turned golden, then reduce the heat to 160–170°C (325–340°F) and carry on cooking until the puff pastry has completely risen. This ensures that the puff pastry will be fully cooked inside.
- ❖ Some kosher whipping creams are thicker and less sweet than non-kosher whipping creams, so if using it in a dessert, I sweeten it with 1 tbsp of icing (confectioners) sugar and thin it with 1 tbsp of milk.
- ❖ Vanilla Instant Pudding is a powder that can be found in Kosher food-shops and on-line. If you can't find it, then for every 250ml (1 cup) whipping cream, add in 75ml (1/4 cup) full-fat milk, 2 tbsp icing sugar and 1 tsp vanilla essence instead.
- ❖ Pareve is the term for food that doesn't contain milk or meat, since in Kosher cooking we don't mix meat and milk or meat and fish.

- ❖ In Jewish recipes, you'll often find that a pareve chicken stock powder is used; it's an important flavouring in the Jewish kitchen. For our grandmothers, chicken stock powder was another spice. In the Kosher kitchen, using a pareve chicken stock powder means that it can be added to fish dishes. If I don't have my home-made stock to hand, then using MSG-free chicken stock powder is a useful substitute.
- ❖ If you want your biscuits and cookies to be extra-crisp and stay fresh for longer, try the following tips when making them:

  For a recipe using icing sugar in the dough, substitute 2 tbsp of the icing sugar for 2 tbsp of caster sugar instead.

  For a butter-based recipe, substitute a quarter of the butter for baking margarine instead.

SHOPPING FOR FOOD

- ❖ I always take care to buy the best ingredients, choosing organic produce when possible.
- ❖ When buying cucumbers and courgettes (zucchini), always choose small, firm ones, as these have the best taste and texture.
- ❖ When choosing an aubergine (eggplant), go for the light, smooth ones, without any blemishes, as these have fewer seeds and are not bitter.
- ❖ When choosing a cabbage, opt for a large one rather than a small one, as it will be sweeter and not bitter.
- ❖ I like to buy fresh garlic, but if that's not available, then I choose the purple-skinned garlic. When cooking with garlic, make sure that the cloves don't have any green parts, as this means the garlic will be bitter.
- ❖ Avoid potatoes which have turned green; these shouldn't be eaten.
- ❖ When shopping for celery, buy the leafy heads as their tasty leaves are excellent in soups and salads.
- ❖ In my recipes, I use full-fat milk and large eggs.

ACKNOWLEDGEMENTS

To my dear mother and father, Shulamit and father Yoav: You inspired my love of cooking by introducing me to the widest variety of dishes and flavours when I was growing up. Thank you for giving me the life every child deserves.

My husband Guy: Thank you for always believing in me and supporting me throughout this whole project. Owing to your great palate and understanding of good food, I was encouraged to experiment in the kitchen and push my culinary boundaries. You have always enjoyed and admired my food, which makes you very rewarding to cook for.

To Manos Chatzikonstantis, my photographer and prop stylist: Thank you for your belief in me and appetite for this project (and my cooking!) from the beginning. Your contribution in producing this book extends so much further than the fabulous photos within it. You are a wonderful person to work with — bringing an infectious enthusiasm, a great eye, a sense of humour and patience to the shoots and me! Your pictures were all so good that it's been very difficult making the final edit!

Jenny Linford, my editor AKA Lightning: Jenny is a great cook and the acclaimed author of best-selling books, including *The Missing Ingredient*, *The London Cookbook*, *Mushrooms* and more. I must say that I couldn't have made it past page two without you, Lightning! Your speed of thought and problem-solving abilities earned you this nickname. Your support and positive reinforcement bolstered my spirit throughout this process. I cannot praise you enough, as you always exceeded my expectations and went the extra mile. I couldn't have asked for a better editor who has since become a dear friend. You helped me to write the stories by expressing my voice through words and to create the recipes with perfect clarity.

Lesley Gilmour, my designer: You are so much fun to work with. You bring a real joie de vivre with you. Your excellent design skills, attention to detail and visual style have made this book look fabulous and totally expressed my vision. Thank you for your genuine enthusiasm for the project. I am thrilled with the results.

Thank you **Metro Publications**, for your knowledge and input.

Thank you **Richard Ehrlich** for your help Americanizing this book. I've really appreciated your food knowledge and your thorough approach. So pleased you enjoyed my cooking!

Akin

Akin: Thank you for being there through it all, for last minute ingredient hunts in the rain and snow! I cannot adequately describe your dedication. Simply put, I couldn't have done it without you.

Gregory Lass: Your knowledge of grammar is so impressive. Thank you for casting your eagle eyes over the stories. I love your positive energy and enthusiasm.

Jonathan Carr: Thank you for your help with the text of the book — I appreciated your poet's eye.

Petya: Thank you for your help prepping the ingredients on photo shoot days. I really appreciate your reliability and the way you get tasks done quickly and efficiently.

SHOPKEEPERS!

Doing the food photography for this book involved a LOT of cooking! I feel very lucky to have such great food shops to source the ingredients from.

Thank you **Hoffman's fish shop** for supplying me so promptly and efficiently with the best fresh fish. And thank you Volkan for your help with the hamsi recipe.

Thank you **Mehadrin Meats** for going the extra mile to always get me the right cuts and delivering them in no time at all! Thank you, too, **Satmar Meats**, for also providing me with great meat and for letting my photographer shoot in your deli.

Thank you **Stoke Newington Green Fruits & Vegetables** for your amazing, colourful selection of fresh fruit and vegetables — and for letting my photographer shoot in your shop.

Frank and Carol, my florists: Thank you for always supplying the right flowers for our photo-shoots. I knew we could count on you every time.

Hoffman's Fish Shop

Florist Frank

Stoke Newington Green Fruits & Veg

Satmar Meats

LIMI'S CHEESE TOAST

Whenever Manos, the photographer, and I arrived at Limi's house to work with her, the first thing she did, with characteristic hospitality, was offer us coffee and breakfast. Scrambled eggs, shakshuka, salads or bourekas were all dishes we enjoyed. A particular favourite, though, was cheese toast, served with Israeli salad, which Limi's mother used to make for her when she was a child. This quickly became a firm favourite of ours and we asked her to put the recipe for it in the book.

Here it is. It's very simple — you take 2 slices of good white bread and layer 2 slices of a hard cheese like Edam on top of one slice of bread, cover it with the other slice then spread butter generously on the top and bottom of the sandwich. Place it in a panini toaster until the bread is golden. Slice it across and diagonally and serve at once while it's piping hot. Thank you, Limi!

Jenny

RECIPE INDEX

TASTE OF TEL AVIV
Tuna Focaccia p.18
Shawarma p.20
Sabich p.23
Green Falafel p.26
Shakshuka p.29
Green Shakshuka p.32
Chicken Shishlik p.36
Our Hamburger p.40
Samis' Bourekas p.43

MEAL IN A BOWL
Fasulya p.50
My Perfect Chicken Soup p.52
Mum's Sweet & Sour Cabbage Soup p.55
Velvet Cauliflower Soup p.56
Broad Bean & Bone Marrow Soup p.58
Easy Tomato Soup p.61
Yoeli's Vegetable Barley Soup p.61
Hearty Red Lentil Soup p.64

DELICIOUS DIPS & RAINBOW SALADS
Hummus p.68
Zhoug p.70
Charred Aubergine (Eggplant) Dip p.71
Moroccan Matbukha p.73
Tzatziki p.74
Toum p.79
Olivier — Russian Potato Salad p.80
Israeli Salad p.82
Coleslaw p.87
Egg Salad p.87
Moroccan Beetroot Salad p.88
Turkish Salad p.88
Quinoa Salad p.90
Leek & Tomato Salad p.93
Cucumber Radish Salad p.93

MY HOME BY THE SEA
Pickled Herrings p.100
Salmon in Spinach Cream Sauce p.103
Baked Fish with a Secret Ingredient p.104
Crispy Home-made Fish Fingers p.107
Nostalgic Kindergarten Fishballs p.108
'MJUJIM' — Married Sardines p.111
Hamsi p.114

QUICK & EASY
Ejja p.122
Potato Latkes p.125
Limi's Schnitzel & Petya's Twist p.128
The Wrap on the Plane p.130
Lemon Paprika Cauliflower p.133
Mum's Perfect Steak p.134
Cumin Spaghetti p.134
Sweet & Sour Courgettes p.136
Courgette Fritters p.139
Syrian Rice with Noodles p.142
Sweet Rice Cakes p.143
New Year Leek Fritters (Karti) p.146
New Year Chard Fritters (Silka) p.148

MY KIDS ARE CRAZY FOR THIS
Yoeli's Stuffed Peppers (Pilep) p.154
Pitta Pizza p.157
Limi's Chicken Curry p.158
Onion Bhaji p.160
Mint Sauce p.160
Egg-Fried Rice p.161
Srulik's Sweet & Sour Chicken p.162
Meatballs Spaghetti p.165
Pancakes p.166
Cookie-Men — Best Chocolate Chip Cookies p.168
Home-made Energy Bars p.171
Limi's Best Ever Home-made Rugelach p.175

SHABBAT SHALOM
Challah p.183
Schenna — Moroccan Chamin p.187
Velvety Orange Chicken p.188
Tahini Dip p.190
Charred Chillies p.192
Moroccan Fish p.196
Braised Lamb Neck p.199
Potato Kugel p.200
Succulent Pot-Roast p.202
Tzimmes p.204
German-Style Potatoes p.204
Apricot-glazed Chicken p.205

THE MILKY WAY
Cottage Cheese & Tomato Lasagne p.210
Smokey Aubergine Cheese Fritters p.212
Borekitas — Cheese Pastries p.216
Greek Salad p.219
Beetroot & Warm Goat's Cheese Salad p.222
Shavuot Cheese Blintzes p.227

BALABUSTE IN THE KITCHEN
Iraqi Beetroot Kubeh Soup p.231
Stuffed Chicken Breast for Tu Bishvat p.234
Meat Kreplach p.239
Stuffed Vine Leaves p.243
Tanzia p.244
Kubeh Nabalsiya p.249
Lamb Buns p.252
Two-Stage Hand-rolled Couscous p.259
Moroccan Mafroum p.260
Chebbakia p.263
Sachertorte p.267
Pistachio Baklava p.270
Rosetta — Almond Syrup p.272

TEA-TIME
Jam Sandwich Cookies p.280
Guraibe p.283
Tahini Cookies p.284
Purim Hamantashcen p.286
Salty-Sweet Butter Herb Biscuits p.291
Chocolate Puff Fingers p.292

DELIGHTFUL DESSERTS
Malabi p.296
70s Compote p.299
Kadaif p.300
Apple Pie p.304
70s Savarin Cake p.306
Snow Ice Cream p.311
Sugar syrup for sorbets p.316
Banana Chocolate Chip Sorbet p.319
Pineapple Mint Sorbet p.322
Strawberry Sorbet p.322

DRINKS
Lemonade p.326
Palooda p.328
Fresh Mint Tea p.331
Hot Chocolate p332
Turkish Coffee p.336
Fruit Smoothies p.336

SWEET MEMORIES
Mum's Torte Cake p.343
Chocolate Roulade p.344
Basbousa 346
Cheese Delkalach p.349
Honey Cake p.352
English Cake p.355
Baked Cream Slices p.356
70s Birthday Cake p.360
Chocolate Coconut Cake p.363
Limi's Carrot Cake p.364
Grandma's Orange Cake p.368
Nostalgic Strawberry Jelly Squares p.371
Easy Nut Torte p.372
Crumb Cheesecake p.375

SHALOM
Peace Cake p.378

SAVOURY BASICS
Soup For Couscous p.384
Quick Couscous p.385
Limi's Rice p.385
Huevos Haminados p.385
Focaccia p.386
Limi's Laffa p.387
Zahtar Pitta p.387
Puffy Falafel Chips p.388
Perfect Chips p.388
Crispy Fried Onion p.388
Preserved Lemons p.389

SWEET BASICS
Sugar Syrup p.390
Home-made Chocolate Rugelach Filling p.391
Rich Blintz Filling p.391
Streusel p.391
Limi's Chocolate Icing (non-dairy) p.391

INDEX

A

Almond
- Almond milk 272
- Almond syrup, Rosetta 272

Anchovies
- Hamsi 114

Apples
- Apple pie 304
- Apple sauce 125

Apricot (dried)
- Beetroot kubeh soup 231
- Stuffed chicken breast 234
- Stuffed vine leaves 243
- Tanzia 244

Apricot jam
- Apricot-glazed chicken 205
- Baked cream slices 356
- Sachertorte 267
- Savarin cake 306
- Sweet & sour chicken 162
- Velvety orange chicken 188

Aubergine (eggplant)
- Charred aubergine (eggplant) dip 71
- Sabich 23
- Smokey aubergine cheese fritters 212

B

Baked cream slices 356
Baklava, Pistachio 270
Banana chocolate chip sorbet 319
Barbecue
- BBQ tips 34
- Chicken shishlik 36

Basbousa 346
Beef
- Beetroot kubeh soup 231
- Fasulya 50
- Kubeh nabalsiya 249
- Lamb buns 252
- Meatballs spaghetti 165
- Meat kreplach 239
- Moroccan mafroum 260
- Perfect steak 134
- Our hamburger 40
- Schenna - Moroccan chamin 187
- Succulent pot-roast 202
- Yoeli's stuffed peppers 154

Beetroot
- Beetroot kubeh soup 231
- Beetroot salad 88
- Beetroot & warm goat's cheese salad 222

Biscuits and Cookies
- Chocolate Chip Cookies 168
- Guraibe 283
- Jam sandwich cookies 280
- Salty-sweet butter herb biscuits 291
- Tahini cookies 284

Blintz
- Rich blintz filling 391
- Shavuot cheese blintzes 227

Borekitas 216
Bourekas 43
Braised lamb neck 199
Bread
- Challah 183
- Focaccia 386
- Laffa 387
- Zahtar Pitta 387

Broad bean and bone marrow soup 58

C

Cabbage,
- Coleslaw 87
- Sweet and sour cabbage soup 55

Cake
- 70s Birthday Cake 360
- Basbousa 346
- Carrot cake 364
- Chocolate coconut cake 363
- Chocolate roulade 344
- Easy nut torte 372
- English cake 355
- Honey cake 352
- Orange cake 368
- Peace cake 378
- Sachertorte 267
- Strawberry jelly squares 371
- Torte cake 343

Carrots
- Carrot cake 364
- Coleslaw 87
- Russian potato salad 80
- Tzimmes 204

Cauliflower
- Lemon paprika cauliflower 133
- Velvet cauliflower soup 56

Challah 183
Chamin (Schenna) 187
Chard fritters 148
Chebbakia 263
Cheese
- Aubergine cheese fritters 212
- Beetroot & warm goat's cheese salad 222
- Blintz filling 391
- Bourekas 43
- Cheesecake 375
- Cheese Delkalach 349
- Cheese pastries (Borekitas) 216
- Cottage cheese & tomato lasagne 210
- Greek salad 219
- Limi's cheese toast 395
- Shavuot cheese blintzes 227

Cheesecake 375
Chicken
- Apricot-glazed chicken 205
- Chicken curry 158
- Chicken shishlik 36
- Chicken soup 52
- Limi's schnitzel 128
- Meatballs spaghetti 165
- Shawarma 20
- Soup for couscous 384
- Stuffed chicken breast 234
- Sweet and sour chicken 162
- Velvety orange chicken 188
- Wrap on the plane 130

Chickpeas
- Green falafel 26
- Hummus 68
- Schenna (Moroccan chamin) 187

Chillies
- Chillies, charred 192
- Zhoug 70

Chips
- Perfect chips 388
- Puffy falafel chips 388

Chocolate
- 70s birthday cake 360
- Banana chocolate chip sorbet 319
- Chocolate chip cookies 168
- Chocolate coconut cake 363
- Chocolate icing (non-dairy) 391
- Chocolate puff fingers 292
- Chocolate roulade 344
- Chocolate rugelach filling 391
- Hot chocolate 332
- Rugelach 175
- Sachertorte 267

Coffee, *See* Turkish coffee
Coleslaw 87
Compote 299
Coriander
- Zhoug 70

Cottage cheese & tomato lasagne 210
Courgettes
- Courgette fritters 139
- Sweet and sour courgettes 136

Couscous
- Quick couscous 385
- Two-stage hand-rolled couscous 259

Cucumbers
- Cucumber radish salad 93
- Greek salad 219
- Israeli salad 82
- Tzatziki 74

Cumin spaghetti 134
Curry, Chicken 158

D

Delkalach 349
Dips
- Charred aubergine (Eggplant) dip p.71
- Hummus p.68
- Mint sauce p.160
- Moroccan matbukha p.73
- Tahini Dip p.190
- Toum p.79
- Tzatziki p.74
- Zhoug p.70

Drinks
Fresh mint tea p.331
Fruit smoothies p.336
Hot chocolate p332
Lemonade p.326
Palooda p.328
Rosetta — almond syrup p.272
Turkish coffee p.336

E

Eggplant, *See* aubergine
Eggs
Egg-fried rice 161
Egg salad 87
Ejja 122
Green shakshuka 32
Huevos haminados 385
Shakshuka 29
Energy bars 171
English cake 355

F

Falafel chips 388
Falafel, Green 26
Fasulya 50
Fish
Baked fish with a secret ingredient 104
Crispy home-made fish fingers 107
Hamsi 114
Mjujim (married sardines) 111
Moroccan fish 196
Nostalgic kindergarten fishballs 108
Pickled herrings 100
Salmon in spinach cream sauce 103
Tuna focaccia 18
Focaccia, *See* Bread
Focaccia, Tuna 18
Fritters
Aubergine cheese fritters 212
Chard fritters (Silka) 148
Courgette fritters 139
Leek fritters (Karti) 146
Potato latkes 125

G

German-style potatoes 204
Goat's cheese salad (& Beetroot) 222
Greek salad 219
Green shakshuka 32
Guraibe 283

H

Hamantashcen 286
Hamburger 40
Hamsi 114
Hanukkah
Chebbakia 263
Potato latkes 125
Herrings, pickled 100
Honey cake 352
Hot chocolate 332
Huevos haminados 385
Hummus 68

I

Ice cream & sorbets
Banana chocolate chip sorbet 319
Pineapple mint sorbet 322
Snow ice cream 311
Sorbets 316
Strawberry sorbet 322
Sugar syrup for sorbets 316
Israeli Salad 82

J

Jam sandwich cookies 280
Jelly Squares 371
Jewish New Year
Honey Cake 352
Leek Fritters (Karti) 146
New Year Chard Fritters (Silka) 148

K

Kadaif 300
Kreplach 239
Kubeh, Beetroot 231
Kubeh Nabalsiya 249
Kugel, Potato 200

L

Laffa 387
Lamb
Braised Lamb Neck 199
Chicken Shishlik 36
Iraqi Beetroot Kubeh Soup 231
Lamb buns 252
Moroccan Mafroum 260
Our Hamburger 40
Shawarma 20
Tanzia 244
Lasagne, cottage cheese & tomato 210
Latkes 125
Leeks
Chicken soup 52
Leek fritters (Karti) 146
Leek & tomato salad 93
Lemonade 326
Lemon paprika cauliflower 133
Lentils, *See* Pulses

M

Mafroum 260
Malabi 296
Marrow, bone
Broad bean & bone marrow soup 58
Fasulya 50
Schenna (Moroccan chamin) 187
Matbukha 73
Meatballs
Meatballs spaghetti 165
Meatballs tip 392
Meat kreplach 239
Sweet & Sour cabbage soup 55
Mint
Fresh mint tea 331
Mint sauce 160
Pineapple mint sorbet 322
Tzatziki 74
Mint sauce 160
Mint Tea 331
Mjujim (married sardines) 111

N

Nuts (almond, pistachio, walnut)
Almond syrup (Rosetta) 272
Nut Torte 372
Pistachio Baklava 270
Nut Torte 372

O

Onion bhaji 160
Onion, crispy fried 388
Orange blossom water
Basbousa 346
Chebbakia 263
Guraibe 283
Kadaif 300
Malabi 296
Pistachio baklava 270
Sugar syrup 390
Oranges
70s compote 299
Chocolate coconut cake 363
Orange cake 368
Orange chicken 188

P

Palooda 328
Pancakes 166
Passover
Broad bean & bone marrow Soup 58
Smokey aubergine cheese fritters 212
Pastries
Borekitas 216
Delkalach 349
Hamantashcen 286
Peace cake 378
Peppers (red, yellow & green)
Peppers, stuffed 154
Pitta pizza 157
Pickled herrings 100
Pineapple mint sorbet 322
Pistachio Baklava 270
Pitta pizza 157
Potatoes
Apricot-glazed chicken 205
Chard fritters 148
German-style potatoes 204
Leek fritters 146
Moroccan mafroum 260
Perfect chips 388
Potato kugel 200
Potato latkes 125
Puffy falafel chips 388
Russian potato salad 80
Pot-roast 202
Preserved lemons 389
Pulses (lentils, chickpeas, broad beans, haricot beans)

Broad bean & bone marrow soup 58
Fasulya 50
Green falafel 26
Hearty red lentil soup 64
Hummus 68
Schenna (Moroccan chamin) 187
Purim
Hamantashcen 286

Q

Quinoa salad 90

R

Rice
Egg-fried rice 161
Limi's rice 385
Stuffed peppers 154
Stuffed vine leaves 243
Sweet rice cakes 143
Sweet & sour cabbage soup 55
Syrian rice with noodles 142
Rosetta (almond syrup) 272
Rosh Hashanah (New Year) 148
Chard fritters (Silka) 148
Honey cake 352
Leek fritters (Karti) 146
Roulade
Chocolate Roulade 344
Peace Cake 378
Rugelach 175

S

Sabich 23
Sachertorte 267
Salads
Beetroot & warm goat's cheese salad p.222
Coleslaw p.87
Cucumber radish salad p.93
Egg salad p.87
Greek salad p.219
Israeli salad p.82
Leek & tomato salad p.93
Moroccan beetroot salad p.88
Olivier — Russian potato salad p.80
Quinoa salad p.90
Turkish salad p.88
Salmon
Baked fish with a secret ingredient 104
Moroccan fish 196
Salmon in spinach cream sauce 103
Salty-sweet butter herb biscuits 291
Sardines, *See* Fish,
Savarin cake 306
Schenna 187
Schnitzel
Wrap on the plane 130
Semolina
Basbousa 346
Beetroot kubeh soup 231
Hand-rolled couscous 259
Shakshuka 29
Shakshuka, Green 32
Shavuot
Cheesecake 375
Delkalach 349
Shavuot cheese blintzes 227
Shawarma 20
Smoothies 336
Snow ice cream 311
Sorbets, *See* Ice cream & sorbets
Soup
Broad bean & bone marrow soup p.58
Chicken soup p.52
Easy tomato soup p.61
Fasulya p.50
Hearty red lentil soup p.64
Iraqi beetroot kubeh soup p.231
Sweet & sour cabbage soup p.55
Velvet cauliflower soup p.56
Vegetable Barley soup p.61
Soup for couscous 384
Sour cream
Basbousa 346
Cheese delkalach 349
Crumb cheesecake 375
Savarin cake 306
Sour cream dip 125
Spaghetti
Cumin spaghetti 134
Meatballs spaghetti 165
Spinach
Green shakshuka 32
Salmon in spinach cream sauce 103
Strawberries
Fruit smoothies 336
Strawberry jelly squares 371
Strawberry sorbet 322
Steak, see Mum's Perfect steak 134
Streusel 391
Stuffed chicken breast 234
Stuffed peppers 154
Stuffed vine leaves 243
Sugar syrup 390
Sugar syrup for sorbets 316
Sweet & sour cabbage soup 55
Sweet & sour chicken 162
Sweet & sour courgettes 136

T

Tahini
Hummus 68
Tahini cookies 284
Tahini dip 190
Tanzia 244
Tartare sauce 107
Tomatoes
Easy tomato soup 61
Israeli salad 82
Leek & tomato salad 93
Matbukha 73
Shakshuka 29
Torte cake 343
Toum 79
Tuna focaccia 18
Turkish coffee 336
Turkish salad 88
Tzatziki 74
Tzimmes 204

V

Vanilla Instant Pudding 392
Vegetable barley soup 61
Vermicelli (lokshen) 52
Chicken soup 52
Lentil soup 64
Vine Leaves, Stuffed 243

Y

Yom Kipur
Chicken soup 52
Kreplach 239

Z

Zahtar pitta 387
Zhoug 70

ABOUT THE AUTHOR

Limi was born in Tel Aviv and lives with her husband and sons in London. Her debut cookbook enshrines a tradition of great family cooking. She continues to perfect recipes both old and new in her own kitchen. Nobody goes hungry in Limi's house.

WWW.LIMICOOKS.COM

Published in 2020 by SavyonPress
savyon.press@gmail.com

Recipes & text by Limi Robinson
Photography & prop styling by Manos Chatzikonstantis
Food styling by Limi Robinson
Edited by Jenny Linford
Design by Lesley Gilmour
Cover design by Lesley Gilmour

Printed and bound in Italy by LEGO.

British Library Cataloguing in Publication Data. A catalogue record for this book is available from the British Library.

ISBN 978-1-5272-4541-9

בני דרום
כרוב כבוש
OSEM
Mini CROUTONS
THE ORIGINAL MINI "MANDEL"
Lieber's
Sadaf
Sadaf
گلاب صدف
(طبیعی)
Natural ROSE WATER
ماء الورد
Zohar Water
MOIR'S
Essence
Vanilla Flavour
FRUTTO E SCIROPPO
OSEM
pudding
VANILLA FLAVOR
80g
100% Tasty
DRIED APRICOTS
HANSON